TEACH YOURSELF
ROCK
THEORY

TEACH YOURSELF
ROCK THEORY

by Steve Tarshis

Amsco Music Publishing Company
New York • London • Tokyo • Sydney • Cologne

For Mom and Dad, Peter and Nancy

Edited by Brenda Murphy
Book design by Mark Stein
Cover design by Iris Weinstein
Cover photo by David Frazier

Photo credits:
p. 9 Bob Gruen
p. 18 courtesy Atlantic Records
p. 29 Barry Levine/Mirage
p. 48 courtesy Warner/Reprise

International Standard Book Number: 0-8256-2204-2
Library of Congress Catalog Card Number: 78-56629

Distributed throughout the world by Music Sales Corporation:

33 West 60th Street, New York 10023
78 Newman Street, London W1
4-26-22 Jingumae, Shibuya-ku, Tokyo 150
27 Clarendon Street, Artarmon, Sydney NSW
Kölner Strasse 199, 5000 Cologne 90

Contents

Foreword

Music theory is misnamed! The study of the way music works (especially how it applies to your guitar) is not theoretical; it's practical.

The how and the why, the construction of chords and voicings, what scales are and what they're for, what intervals are—these are a few of the areas that can clear up the "mystery" of music. It's no mystery. It's a jigsaw puzzle, but all the pieces fit together. That's what this book is about: putting the pieces together, specifically for the guitarist.

An understanding of theory is an invaluable tool—not just for playing, but for songwriting, composing, arranging, and just all around musicianship. It doesn't matter whether you're a straight rocker, or a mellow player, or just like music no matter what the style. When you know how music works you can learn what the components of any particular style are, so then you can play what you *want*, not just what you *can.*

This book can be used even if you're not very familiar with written music. In fact, this book should help you to become more comfortable with written notation because it's aimed directly at the guitarist. All the examples are in guitar tablature as well as standard notation.

So what is a thirteenth chord? And what is a third or a sixth? How do you know what to play when the music says "G" but you're tired of the same old chords? Read on, read on.

We're going to begin our study of theory with the names of the notes and a look at intervals. This may not exactly warm your rock-and-roll heart, but some knowledge of intervals is absolutely essential to any understanding of music. A little later in the book we'll be getting into a lot of interesting chords and progressions. So hang in there and follow it through.

Intervals

The Chromatic Scale

Musical notes are named alphabetically, from A to G. Since there are twelve tones in all in our Western music system, sharps (♯) and flats (♭) are used to expand the original seven letter names to cover the notes between them. When all these notes are arranged in consecutive order, this is called a *chromatic scale*.

Chromatic Scale:

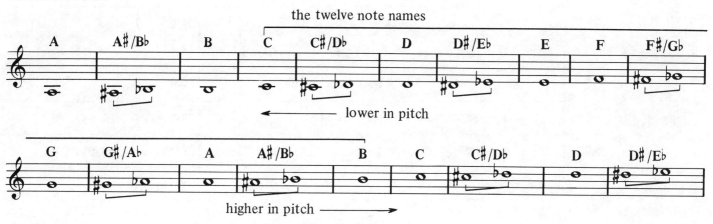

In the above scale, you'll notice that some notes are in pairs (A♯/B♭ or C♯/D♭). In these cases, both spellings and both notes apply to the same pitch. For instance, if you finger B♭ on the fifth string, first fret of your guitar, you're also playing A♯. Similarly, C♯ played on the second fret of the second string is the same as D♭. Notes which can have another spelling are called *enharmonic*.

Here are some examples of enharmonic notes.

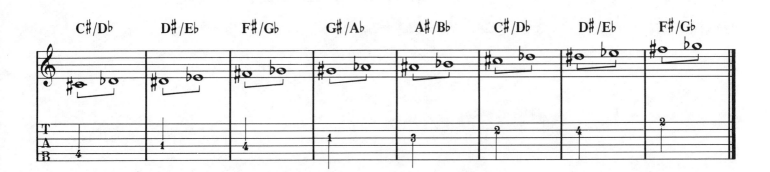

Although there are only twelve different tones in Western music, there are many other possible notes, due to repetition in different registers. Moving up (or down) the chromatic scale, the distance between any note and the next nearest note with the same letter name is the interval of an *octave*. (A good definition of an *interval* is the distance between two notes, counting the first note as "1.") The guitar has a range of over three octaves—more than most instruments. (The piano is king, comprising over seven octaves.)

The next diagram shows all the notes that can be played on each string of the guitar. You probably already know that on the guitar, the same pitch may be fingered several ways. For example, the C on the second string, first fret, produces the same sound as the C on the third string, fifth fret. The note C on the fifth string, third fret, however, is an octave lower. The C on the first string, eighth fret is an octave higher. Play all of these C's and *sing* them and you'll hear exactly what I mean.

← Frets →

Strings		1	2	3	4	5	6	7	8	9	10	11	12	13	14	15
1st	E	F	F#/Gb	G	G#/Ab	A	A#/Bb	B	C	C#/Db	D	D#/Eb	E	F	F#/Gb	G
2nd (thin)	B	C	C#/Db	D	D#/Eb	E	F	F#/Gb	G	G#/Ab	A	A#/Bb	B	C	C#/Db	D
3rd	G	G#/Ab	A	A#/Bb	B	C	C#/Db	D	D#/Eb	E	F	F#/Gb	G	G#/Ab	A	A#/Bb
4th	D	D#/Eb	E	F	F#/Gb	G	G#/Ab	A	A#/Bb	B	C	C#/Db	D	D#/Eb	E	F
5th	A	A#/Bb	B	C	C#/Db	D	D#/Eb	E	F	F#/Gb	G	G#/Ab	A	A#/Bb	B	C
6th (thick)	E	F	F#/Gb	G	G#/Ab	A	A#/Bb	B	C	C#/Db	D	D#/Eb	E	F	F#/Gb	G

Let's take a look at the diagram. Notice that on each string, an octave occurs between the open position and the twelfth fret. The distance between any two notes next to one another on the guitar is one half step (or one fret in either direction). The half step is the smallest intervallic unit of Western music. Every note is separated from its neighbor by one half step.

```
        1/2step   1/2       1/2       1/2       1/2       1/2       1/2
      C  C#    D  Eb    E  F  F#    G  Ab    A  Bb    B  C  C#    D  Eb   etc.
   1/2 step   1/2       1/2       1/2       1/2       1/2       1/2       1/2
```

4

The Octave

An *octave* is formed by two notes which are separated by twelve half steps, or eight scale steps. (See the Appendix in the back of this book for an explanation of Scales.)

Let's play some octaves on the guitar.

Octaves:

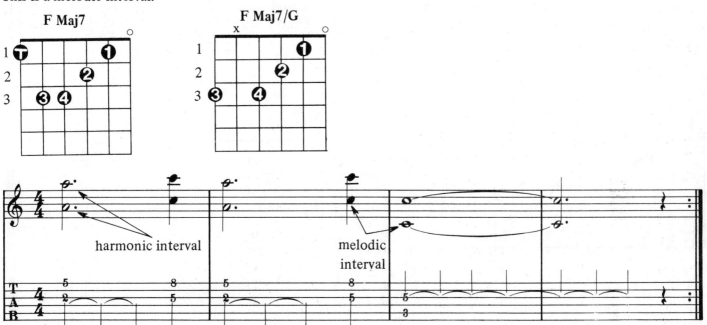

You can probably hear that both notes of an octave sound the same. The only difference between them is pitch: One of the notes is higher than the other.

The sound of the octave is heard frequently in guitar music. A melody played in octaves has a strong, jazzy sound, one that is immediately identified with such guitarists as Wes Montgomery and George Benson. Let's look at the following example of a melody played in octaves, in the jazz-rock, fusion style. In this example octaves are used in two ways. When two notes are played simultaneously they form a *harmonic interval*. When notes are played in sequence, as part of a melody, they form a *melodic interval*. In this example, each note of the melody is doubled at the octave. This is a harmonic interval. The distance between the note at the end of the second measure, and the note at the beginning of the third measure is an octave. This is a melodic interval.

Make sure you play through the example. Get a friend to play the chords while you play the melody, and then change parts.

The Unison

Two notes that are exactly the same in pitch and letter name are called a *unison.* You use the unison when you tune the guitar. The second string fingered on the fifth fret produces an E, the same pitch as the open first string. These two notes are said to be "in unison."

The Perfect Fifth

Aside from the unison or octave, the next strongest interval relationship is the *perfect fifth.* A perfect fifth is formed by two notes which are seven half steps (or five scale steps) apart. The distance from C up to G is a perfect fifth, as shown below. From A♭ up to E♭ and from D down to G are also perfect fifths. These may be abbreviated, ↑P5 and ↓P5.

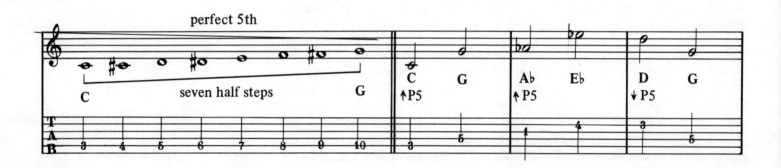

Rock players often use just perfect fifths, instead of full chords, to achieve a basic rock and roll or heavy metal sound. The next example is a rock progression in fifths.

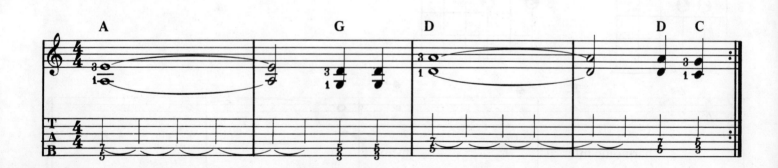

The Perfect Fourth

The inversion of a perfect fifth is a *perfect fourth*. (That is, from C up to G is a perfect fifth, but from G up to C is a perfect fourth.) The notes of a perfect fourth are five half steps (or four scale steps) apart.

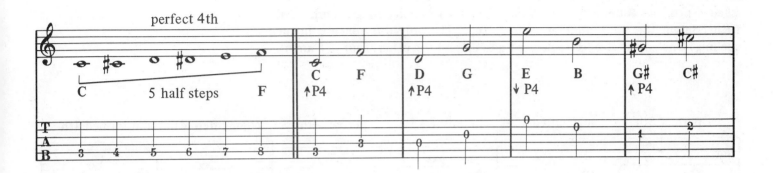

The perfect fourth is the interval between all the open strings of the guitar, with the exception of the major third between the second and third strings. The example below shows the melodic perfect fourth, found in the famous opening of "Pinball Wizard" by The Who.

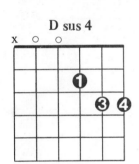

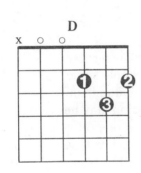

Milatary Taps

Augmented and Diminished Intervals

The interval of the fifth has two variations. The perfect fifth contains seven half steps. The *diminished fifth* contains one less half step (six); the *augmented fifth*, one more (eight). Remember: Whatever type of fifth it is, it still must contain five different letter names.

The interval of the fourth has the same variations. The perfect fourth contains five half steps. The *augmented fourth* has six half steps, and the *diminished fourth* has four. Notice that the augmented fourth and the diminished fifth contain the same number of half steps. The only difference is in the spelling: One covers five letter names (a fifth) and the other, four (a fourth).

perfect 5th	augmented 5th	diminished 5th	perfect 4th	augmented 4th	diminished 4th
7 half steps	8 half steps	6 half steps	5 half steps	6 half steps	4 half steps
C G	C G♯	C G♭	C F	C F♯	C F♭ (E)

The Tritone

The interval containing six half steps (the diminished fifth or augmented fourth) is also referred to as a *tritone*, because it covers three whole steps. This is a very special interval. It is the essential component of all dominant seventh chords—C7, D7, E7, etc. In fact, an entire blues progression may be played using only tritones, as shown below. Many guitarists use this technique when they "comp" the blues. Play this example with a friend or tape machine playing the full chords, or just a simple bass line, to get the effect of these tritones.

John Lennon and Elton John

Thirds

Next we come to the interval which comprises three scale steps, the *third*. A *major third* is formed by two notes that are four half steps apart. A *minor third* is formed by two notes that are three half steps apart.

Repeated thirds are found in the guitar breaks of such early rock and roll masters as Chuck Berry, and Bill Haley and the Comets. (Listen to the guitar solo in "Rock Around the Clock.") In the next example major and minor thirds are used in this way. Don't forget that the best way to play these examples is with the chords as accompaniment. Use a tape recorder or a friend, and play both parts!

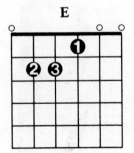

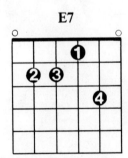

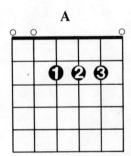

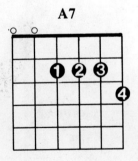

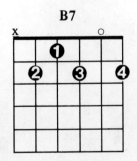

Fifties Style

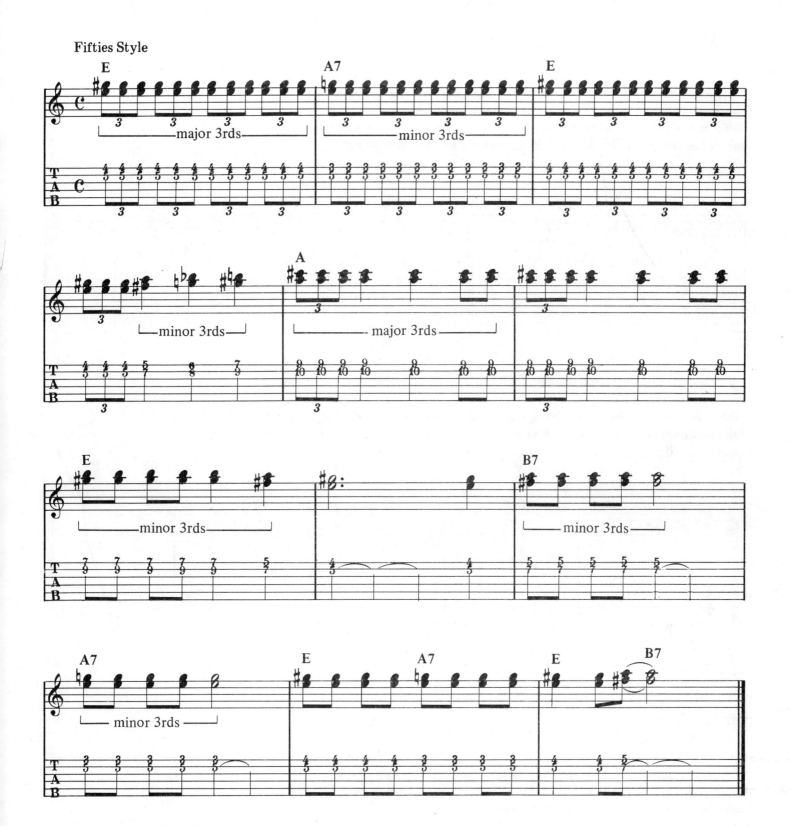

Sixths

The inversion of a third is a *sixth* of the opposite quality. For instance, the inversion of a minor third is a *major sixth* and the inversion of a major third is a *minor sixth*. A sixth of any variety comprises six scale steps, but the major sixth includes nine half steps and the minor sixth, eight.

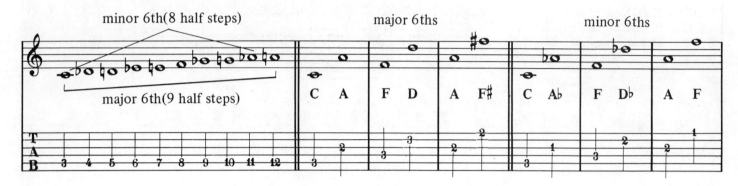

On the guitar, the sound of major and minor sixths is often heard in country and country-rock music. This interval, especially when played on the higher strings, has the sweet, lonesome sound of the pedal steel guitar. Try this next example with an easy country-rock feel and you'll see what I mean.

Seconds

Another name for our basic unit, the half step, is a *minor second*. As you might have guessed, there is also an interval called a *major second* which comprises two half steps (or one whole step).

Many melodies are made up almost entirely of seconds. Let's play the first few measures of "With a Little Help from My Friends" by the Beatles.

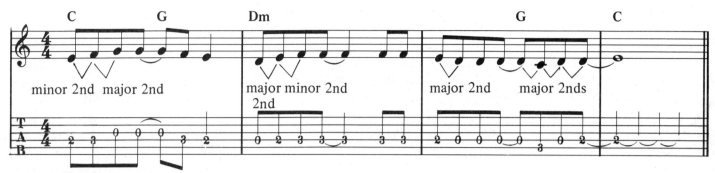

Sevenths

The inversion of a second is a *seventh* of the opposite quality. A *major seventh* has only one less half step than an octave, eleven. A *minor seventh* contains ten half steps.

Interval Spelling

It's very possible that at this point you are a little confused as to how to account for sharps and flats when counting half steps. A simple rule to remember is that you must move one letter name for every number of the interval to be found. For example, if you want a major seventh up from D, you must count seven letters up from D: D,E,F,G,A,B,C. Now we know that the top note must be a C of some kind. By looking at the Chromatic Scale chart and figuring the right number of half steps for a major seventh (eleven) we arrive at C♯/D♭. Since we know that we must have a C of some kind, C♯ is the correct answer. A minor sixth up from C is . . .? Count six letters up from C (counting C as "1"): C,D,E,F,G,A. Looking at the Chromatic Scale chart we find that a minor sixth up from C is eight half steps away— G♯ or A♭. Since we know that the proper name is an A of some sort, we choose A♭. A minor sixth up from C is A♭.

Getting back to practical applications, we find that the interval of the minor seventh is a real staple of funk music, as in the following example.

13

That about covers our introduction to intervals. If you can get a grasp on intervals you're a long way down the road to understanding theory. Try to stick with it, play the examples and go over the things that seem hard to understand. The more you deal with this material the easier it will get. The same applies to music notation.* I hope you're trying to deal with that language too. Learning to read and write music, even on an elementary level, will put you miles ahead in understanding music. Let's also face the fact that you may be now, or in the future, competing against other musicians, and really knowing music is always an advantage.

The following chart sums up our study of intervals.

Interval		Half Steps	Example
2nd	minor	1	C = D♭
	major	2	C = D
3rd	minor	3	C = E♭
	major	4	C = E
4th	diminished	4	C = F♭ (E)
	perfect	5	C = F
	augmented	6	C = F♯
5th	diminished	6	C = G♭
	perfect	7	C = G
	augmented	8	C = G♯
6th	minor	8	C = A♭
	major	9	C = A
7th	minor	10	C = B♭
	major	11	C = B
octave	perfect	12	C = C

*See the Appendix on Notation for a review of the basics.

14

Basic Chords

Chords are fundamental and essential to the guitarist. A thorough knowledge of chords will give you the command of your instrument that you need to "flow" with the music and not be fighting against its current. As you come to understand how chords work, you will begin to see how music works. Lines, parts, leads and riffs—all the things that a rock guitarist brings to a band—are based on a knowledge of harmony. And harmony means chords.

The next thing that we are going to do is learn how to "spell" different kinds of chords and play them on the guitar. When you are confronted with basic chords, such as C or Am, you should know how to play them in the right place on the guitar to get the sound that you are looking for. More complex chords, (Am9, C_9^6, Fm7$\flat$ 5) shouldn't throw you when you understand what their names mean and how you can build them yourself on your instrument. This is the kind of thing we're going to cover in this chapter—the tools of the trade.

Chord Qualities

The two basic types of chords are *major chords* and *minor chords*. "Major" and "minor" refer to the quality of a chord. Major chords seem to have a bright, happy, powerful sound. Minor chords can be described as sad, mysterious or spiritual. Of course, these words are just guidelines and not really adequate to describe the experience of music, but I'm sure you get the idea.

Play the following chords and listen to the different qualities.

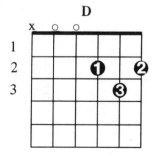

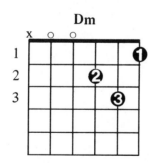

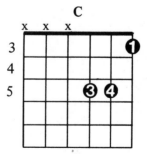

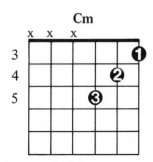

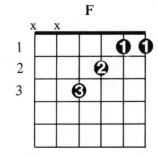

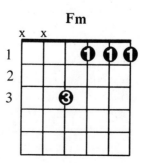

The letter name of a chord tells us what the *root* is. For example, the root of an A minor chord is A. The root of a C chord is C. (Major chords are often described by the letter name alone. A "D" chord is the same as a D Major chord.) The root of a chord is the foundation on which the other notes of a chord are built. The root is the most prominent note in a chord; the one you hear most strongly. A bass player uses the roots of chords as the basis for his part.

Major and minor chords (*triads*) both contain three main notes. These are the *root*, the *fifth* and the *third*. The third of the chord is the only one of the three parts that changes, affecting the quality of the chord: When the third is major, the chord is major; and when the third is minor, the chord is minor. For instance, an A Major chord and an A minor chord have the same root and fifth. Only the thirds are different.

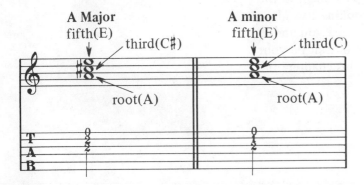

The Major Chord

In building a *major chord* we have already seen that the root of any chord is the same note as its letter name. The root of an A Major chord is A. The fifth is found by locating the note that is a fifth up from A. This note is E.

The only remaining part is the third. For an A Major chord we need to add the note that is a major third up from the root, A. That note is C♯. Now we have the three notes that form an A chord: A (root), E (fifth) and C♯ (major third). Any place that we play these notes on the guitar we are playing an A chord.

Try out these different ways to play an A chord.

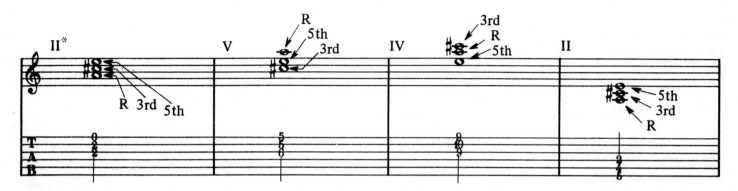

*Roman numerals show what fret (position) the notes start on.

Doubling

You should realize, of course, that most of the chords you play on the guitar contain more than three notes. The three notes of the basic triad are often *doubled*. That is, one or more of them will be played again in another octave. The root and fifth are the notes most often doubled, for this produces the most powerful sound.

The following chords are examples of some full-sounding voicings used by rhythm guitarists to achieve a large sound that really "covers." All three are shown as A Major chords, but they are movable—that is, they may be moved up and down the neck chromatically to get different chord names. Moving one of these A chords up one fret will produce a Bb chord. Moving up three frets will give you a C chord, and so on. Each of these three chords may be played on any fret, so that in this way you can play any major chord.

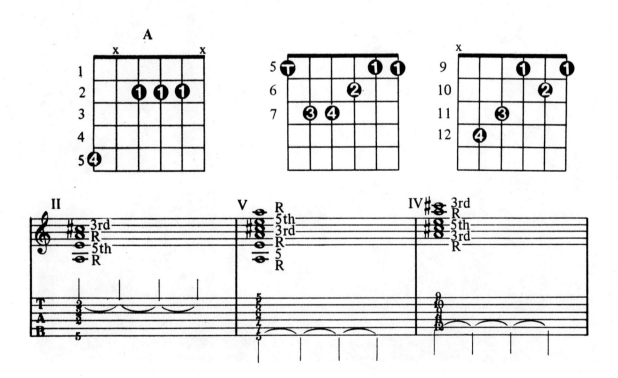

The next example shows how some full-sounding chords are used in achieving a heavy metal sound. The fingerings for these chords are the same as those we saw above, except this time they have been moved around the neck. Try to pick out the root, fifth and third of each chord. Don't forget to take the repeats. When you see these signs (   ), it means that the notes they enclose should be played once more. An accent (>) means that that note or chord is to be played strongly, with authority. When you play this next example, think of The Who or Aerosmith.

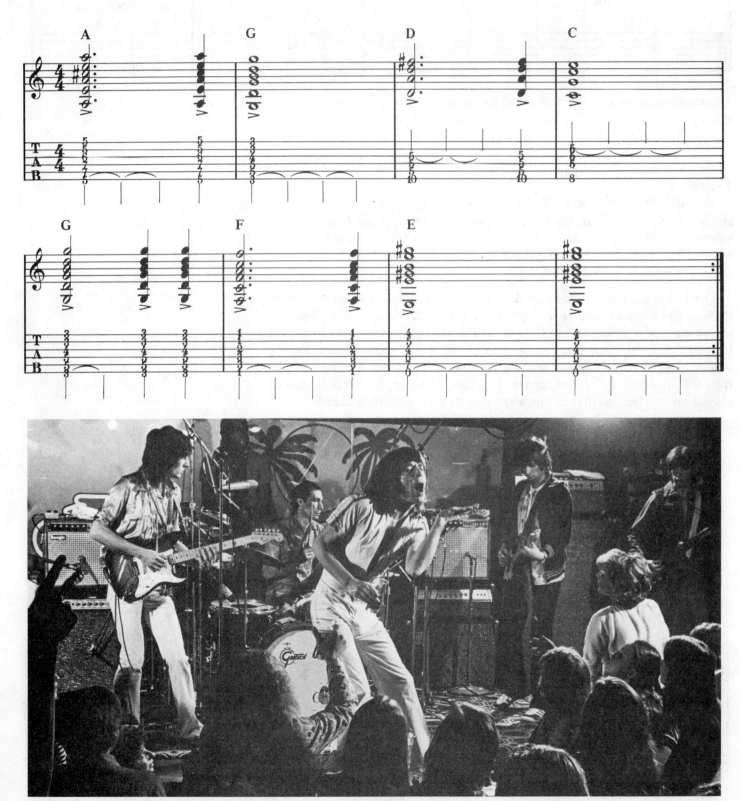

The Rolling Stones at El Macombo

The Minor Chord

Minor chords are constructed in the same way as major chords, except that the minor third takes the place of the major third. The components of an A minor chord are the root, A (same as the chord name), the fifth, E (a fifth up from the root) and the minor third, C (a minor third up from the root).

A minor

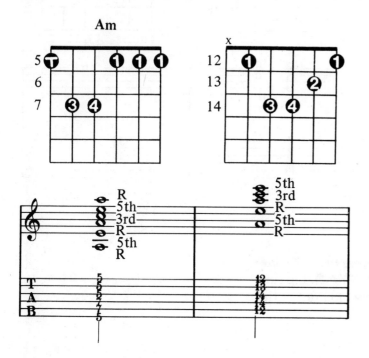

Like major chords, minor chords often have doubled notes, especially the root and the fifth. Here are some strong, full-sounding A minor chords. The second of these chords is on the twelfth fret, so you may have trouble fingering it if you're not playing on an electric guitar with cut-away sides. Don't worry though, both chords are movable, and may be played up and down the neck to get all of the minor chords.

Let's construct a few more major and minor chords.

First, a major triad on C. The root of a C chord is the same as its letter name, C; the fifth is a fifth up from C, G; the major third is four half steps up from C, E. Therefore, a C Major chord is spelled C-E-G.

C Major

Any C, E, and G played together on the guitar constitutes a C Major chord. Different doublings may be used to increase the number of possible C chords. Here are a few of these. Some of them are full-sounding chords, and some are "small-note voicings" which are used for lead work, solos, etc. Work these out and then try to find your own voicings. This is one of the best ways to really get to know the neck of the guitar.

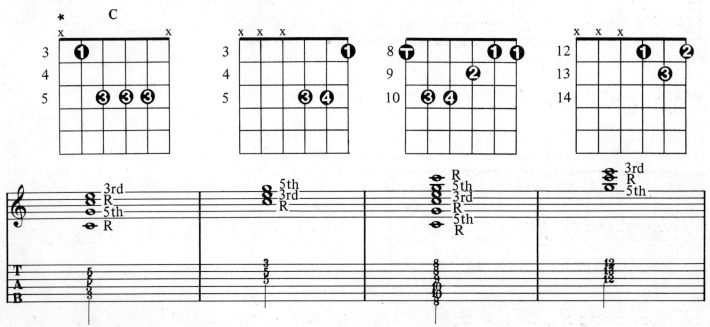

*This is an excellent hard rock voicing.

To play a C minor chord, we can retain the root (C) and the fifth (G), but we now use the minor third, E♭ (three half steps above the root). I'm sure you've noticed that the difference between a major and minor chord of the same letter name is only one half step.

C minor

20

Various doublings increase the number of C minor chords we can construct on the guitar. Here are some full-sounding chords and some small-note voicings.

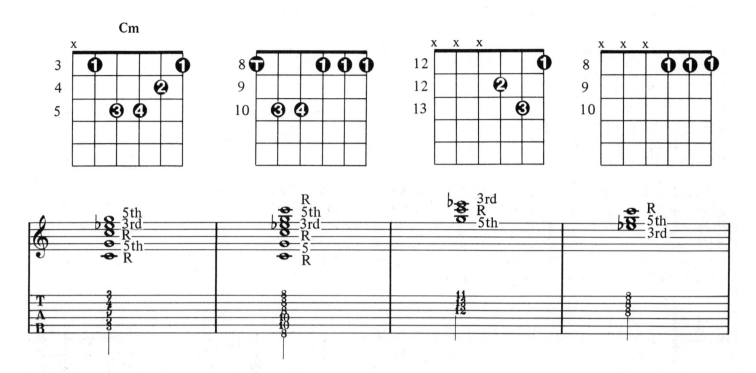

Major and Minor Chords in Progressions

Now, let's put some of this information to good use and make some rock and roll. Suppose we have this medium tempo chord progression.

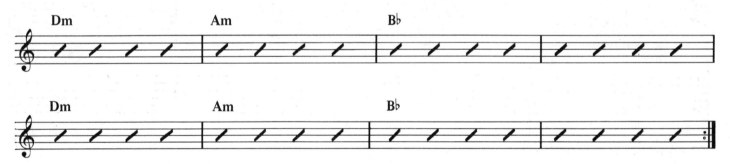

Let's spell out all of the chords so that we have our raw material. The D minor chord consists of the root, D (same as the letter name), the fifth, A (seven half steps up from the root) and the minor third, F (three half steps above the root). The A minor chord (as we've already seen) is made up of the root (A), the fifth (E) and the minor third (C). A B♭ chord contains the root (B♭), the fifth (F) and the major third (D).

Using this information we'll come up with several different guitar parts that could be played, alone or together. First, here's a rhythm guitar part consisting of "fat" (full-sounding) chords.

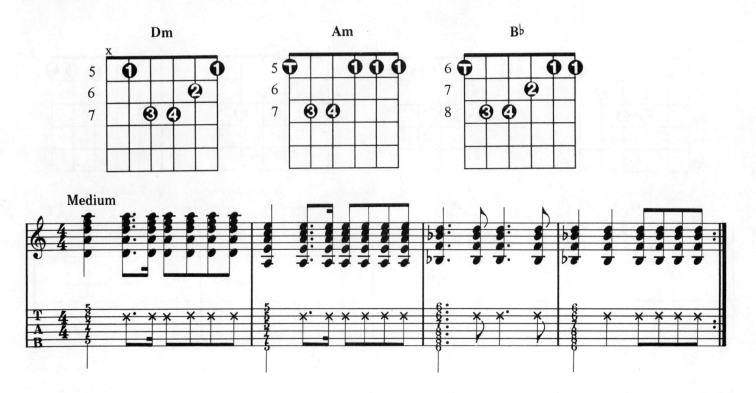

Over this part, another guitar could be playing accent chords made up of small-note voicings. Notice that these small-note voicings are the top notes of full-sounding chords.

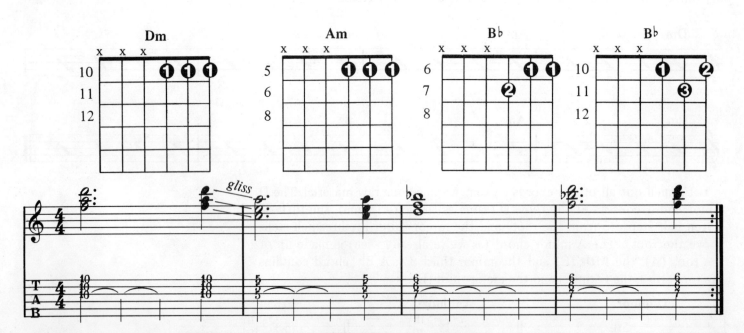

The *gliss* in the second bar is short for *glissando.* This effect is produced by striking the first chord (or note) and then sliding the fingers up (or down) the guitar neck to the second chord. The sound is similar to that of the pedal steel guitar. You can hear this effect in the introduction to "Band on the Run" by Paul McCartney and Wings.

We can get another lead guitar part by using the same small-note voicings, but playing them *arpeggio* style. This means that instead of playing the chord notes simultaneously, as we did above, we will play them one at a time. This technique is used often by guitarists to make an interesting part out of a simple chord progression. Below is an example, using the same progression we've been working with and the same small-note voicings we used in the last example. When you play these arpeggios, finger the chord as you did in the last example, and hold your fingers down while you strike the indicated notes so that they ring out.

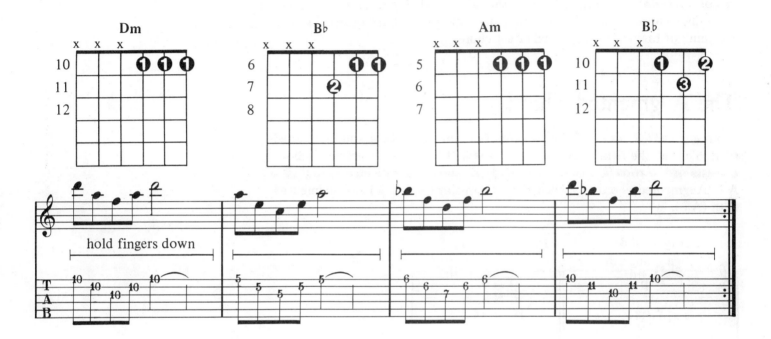

Try to play these different parts together with a friend or tape recorder to get an idea how they sound together. Then try the whole process with other chord progressions. The way to really get the neck down is to be thinking constantly about voicings and notes with the guitar in your hand. This will be work at first, but the more you do it the more it will become second nature. As these things become a part of you, you'll be on your way to becoming a proficient guitarist and musician.

Augmented and Diminished Chords

Major and minor are the two basic chord qualities. There are two kinds of "color" chords, however, that can be thought of as being variations of major and minor chords. These are the *augmented* and the *diminished* chords. You can think of them as being special effect chords.

The Augmented Chord

An *augmented chord* can be thought of as a major triad with an augmented fifth. That is, the fifth is expanded by one half step. A C Augmented chord consists of the root (C), the major third (E) and the augmented fifth (G♯). A D Augmented chord is spelled root (D), major third (F♯) and augmented fifth (A♯).

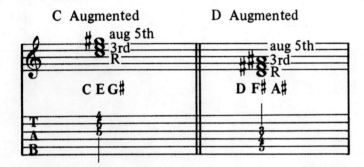

The augmented chord is sometimes heard in introductions. A well-known example is the Beatles' "Oh Darlin'." Augmented chords can be played on the guitar with both small-note voicings and full-sounding chords.

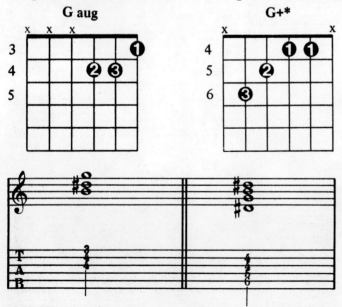

*A plus sign (+) is often used to indicate an augmented chord.

In the next example I've written out a chord progression containing an augmented triad. Notice that the G Augmented acts as a kind of passageway between the G and the C chords. This is called a *passing chord*, and the augmented chord often functions in this way. This chord progression is to be played at a slow tempo like an Elton John or Beatles ballad. The lead part consists entirely of *chord tones* (notes contained in the spelling of the chord) in small-note voicings. Notice that some of these voicings do not contain all three chord members. Instead, they consist of various two-note combinations: root and fifth, third and fifth, and root and third. (We used the root-and-fifth combination in the section on Intervals.) The chord boxes below show good full-sounding voicings that may be used for the rhythm guitar parts.

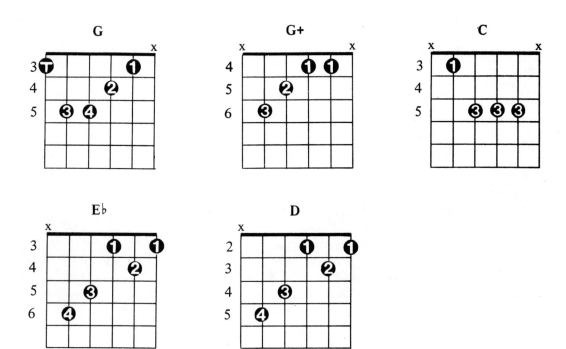

The lead part sounds best when played with a very electric, rock sound on the guitar. (Use your treble or lead pick-up.)

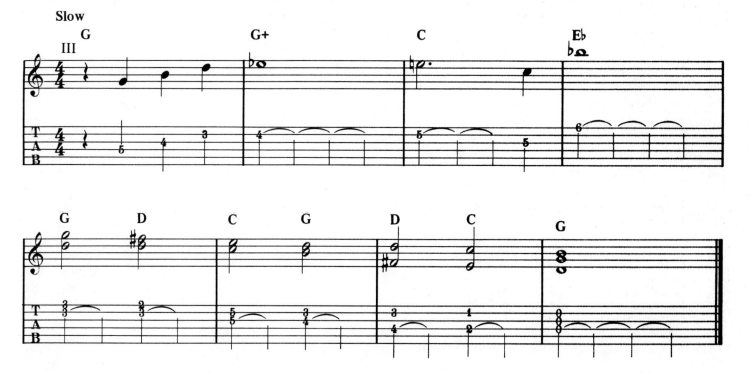

The Diminished Chord

A *diminished chord* may be thought of as a minor triad with a diminished fifth. A C diminished chord consists of the root (C), the minor third (E♭) and the diminished fifth (G♭). An E diminished chord is spelled E (root), G (minor third) and B♭ (diminished fifth).

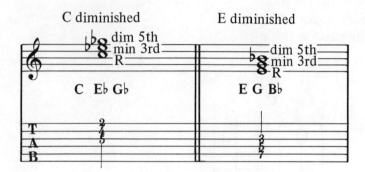

The Diminished Seventh Chord

In rock and pop music, the diminished chord is almost never used without the addition of the *diminished seventh* above the triad (eight half steps up from the root), resulting in the *diminished seventh chord.* Because to qualify as a seventh (whatever type) this interval must cover seven letter names (C, D, E, F, G, A, B), its technical name is B♭♭. But it is much easier to use its enharmonic spelling, A. Therefore, a C diminished seventh chord is spelled C (root), E♭ (minor third), G (diminished fifth) and A (enharmonic spelling of the diminished seventh, B♭♭). Using the same method, an E diminished seventh chord is spelled E-G-B♭-C♯.

As you can see, this is an unusual chord and I don't want you to get too hung up on the theorectical side of it and ignore its very practical uses. The diminished seventh chord has the peculiarity of repeating itself every three frets. This means that if you play a C diminished seventh chord on the third fret, you may move the whole voicing up three frets and you will be playing another C diminished seventh chord. Moving up another three frets will have the same result. This means that one voicing will give you a lot of yardage on the neck. The reason for this is that a diminished seventh chord can be named for any one of the notes contained in its spelling. So, if you play a C diminished seventh chord (C-E♭-G♭-A) you are also playing an E♭ diminished seventh chord, a G♭ diminished seventh chord and an A diminished seventh chord. An E diminished seventh chord (E-G-B♭-C♯) yields diminished seventh chords on G, B♭ and C♯. Pretty good for not even moving your hands. Now let's look at some voicings.

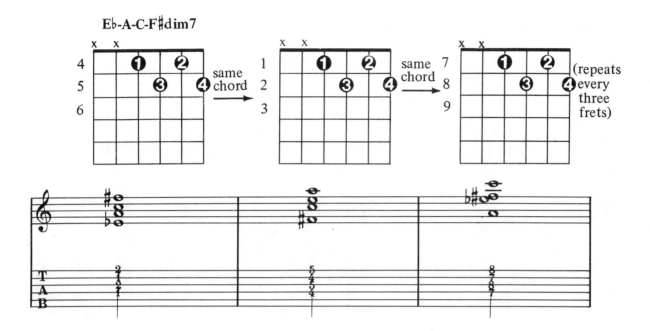

E♭-A-C-F♯dim7

same chord

same chord

(repeats every three frets)

If you work out the spellings, you will discover that any diminished seventh chord will yield four complete diminished seventh chords, each one having root, minor third, flatted fifth and diminished seventh (or major sixth, the same thing).

Here's another, fuller diminished seventh voicing. It repeats every three frets too.

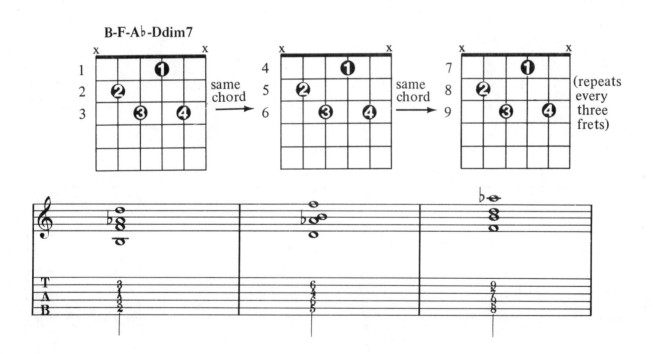

B-F-A♭-Ddim7

same chord

same chord

(repeats every three frets)

Progressions with Diminished Chords

A much used rag-time progression, heard in such songs as "Alice's Restaurant" by Arlo Guthrie, contains rising diminished chords.

In the song "We are the Champions," by Queen, the diminished seventh
chords give the song a classical flavor.

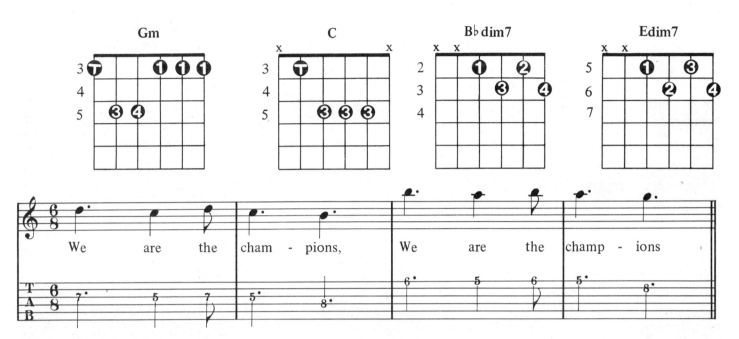

Freddie Mercury of Queen

Seventh Chords

So far, with the exception of the diminished chords, we have dealt only with triads—chords that have three different notes (not counting doublings). We can add interest and color to these chords by adding another note. The most frequent addition is the *seventh*.

The Dominant Seventh Chord

In rock music the most common kind of seventh chord we find is the *dominant seventh chord*, such as E7, A7, C7 and D7. To form a dominant seventh chord, we start with a major triad and then add above it a minor seventh (ten half steps up from the root). So, to build a C7 chord, we take the root (C), the perfect fifth (G), the major third (E)—a C Major triad, so far—and we add to that the note a minor seventh above the root. This note is B♭.

Let's build an A♭ 7. First we spell an A♭ Major chord: root (A♭), major third (C), fifth (E♭). Then we add the minor seventh, G♭ (ten half steps up from the root).

Inversions

So far, we've been finding the minor seventh of a chord by counting ten half steps up. There is another way to think of this: *inversion*. Instead of counting ten half steps up, we can find the same note by counting two half steps down, a major second. The inversion of a minor seventh is a major second. This diagram of the chromatic scale shows how to find a minor seventh up from A by going a major second down from A.

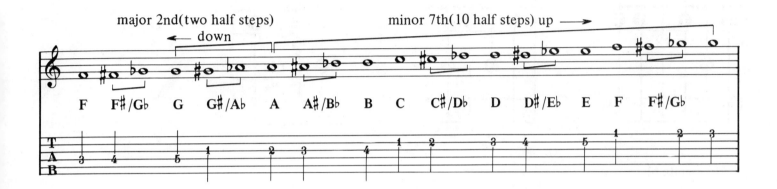

Below are some voicings for a C7 chord. Anywhere on the guitar that we play the notes C-E-G-Bb (in any order) we are playing a C7 chord. These various orders in which we may spell a C7 (C-E-G-Bb , E-G-Bb -C, G-Bb -C-E, etc.) are the *inversions* of the C7 chord.

Not all C7 chords contain all four notes. The only notes you really need to indicate a dominant seventh chord are the third and the seventh. So, some small-note voicings of a dominant seventh chord may be missing the root or the fifth. In the case of C7, the "vital" notes are E (the third) and Bb (the seventh). The root (C) is not absolutely necessary (one reason is that the bass player usually covers the root of a chord) and neither is the fifth (G).

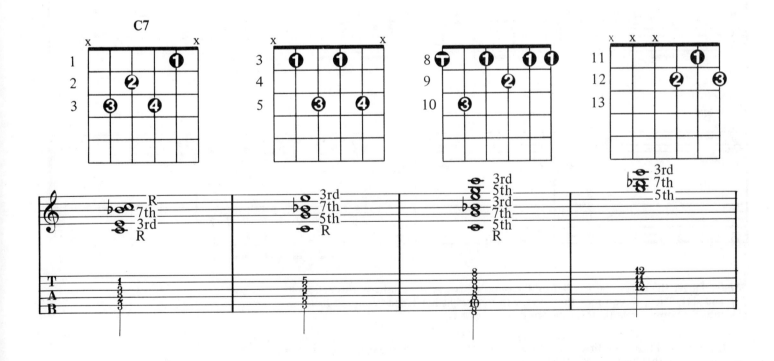

One of the most common uses of dominant seventh chords in our music is in the blues. In fact, the presence of a dominant seventh chord will give any song (even one that is not a blues in the strict sense) a bluesy feeling. Here is the classic blues progression in the key of A. I've written out a lead part that is based on chord tones and small-note voicings. (For a full treatment of blues see my book on *Lead Guitar.*)

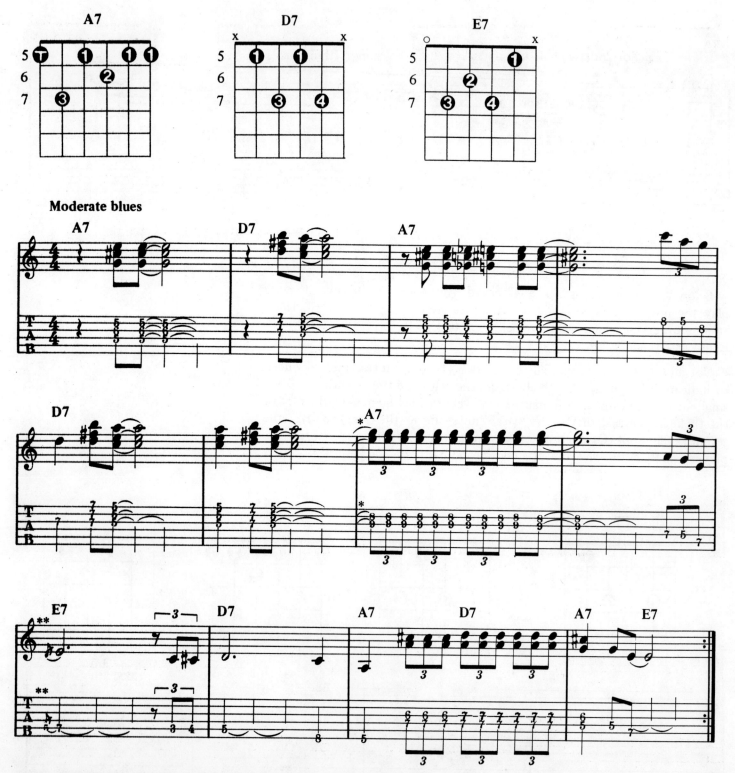

Moderate blues

Slide: Finger the notes one fret before the ones written in the music (in this case, frets five and six). Then, as you pick the notes with your right hand, slide your left-hand fingers into the correct frets (in this case, frets six and seven).

**Hammer-on:* Finger the first note written, the grace note, and as you pick with your right hand, rapidly "hammer-on" the second note.

In this excerpt from Elton John's classic "Philadelphia Freedom," you can see how the presence of dominant seventh chords injects a bluesy, gospel, soul feeling into the song.

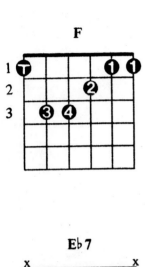
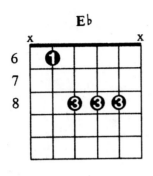
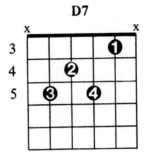
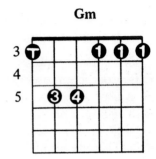

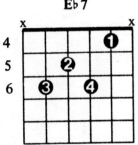
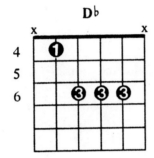
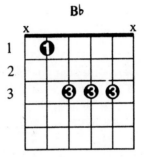

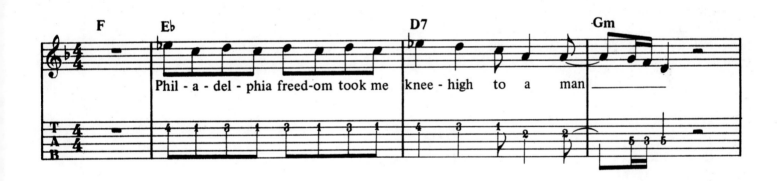

Phil - a - del - phia freed-om took me knee - high to a man____

Yeah! Gave me peace of mind__ my dad - dy nev - er had

Resolution

Dominant seventh chords often function as the "lead-in" chords of a chord progression. This is because they have a natural tendency to go to another chord. The chord that they want to resolve to is the one that is a perfect fourth up. For example, a C7 naturally resolves to an F chord (major or minor). A B7 tends to resolve to an E chord. Look at the excerpt from "Philadelphia Freedom" and notice how the D7 chord in the third measure goes to the G minor. Play this resolution, and the ones I just mentioned, on your guitar so you can hear what I mean.

Of course, a dominant seventh chord does not always resolve in this way. Often the composer will purposely *not* use this resolution because it has been used so often in the past, in both classical and popular idioms. In the fifth measure of "Philadelphia Freedom" the Eb 7 goes to D7, and then the D7 goes to Db . Here Elton John has chosen to move the chords down a half step. This is a common alternative to the classic resolution, up a fourth.

In the next example we have a hard rock progression that uses the perfect fourth resolution of a dominant chord. The C♯ 7 chord is used at the end of the cycle to lead back to F♯ and start the cycle again. You've got to take the repeats to get the feeling of resolution. This example should be played with drive and intensity, similar to "Train Kept A Rollin'," Aerosmith version.

Over some notes of the lead part, the sign that looks like a lightning bolt indicates that those notes are to be played with vibrato. *Vibrato* is a great lead guitar effect that is played in this way: After you've plucked the note with your right hand, hold the note with your left-hand finger and move that finger up and down (at right angles to the neck, not side to side as in the classical guitar vibrato). Some players take the whole hand off the neck, leaving only the finger touching the string and vibrating it. This effect requires a lot of practice, so you've got to build up those finger muscles. Listen to other guitarists on records (or live) to get an idea of what kind of vibrato you want. There are as many sounds to this effect as there are guitarists! Hint: The speed of the finger doing the vibrato will largely affect the kind of sound produced. It should not be too fast.

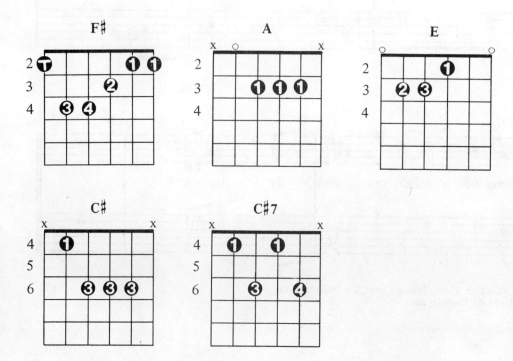

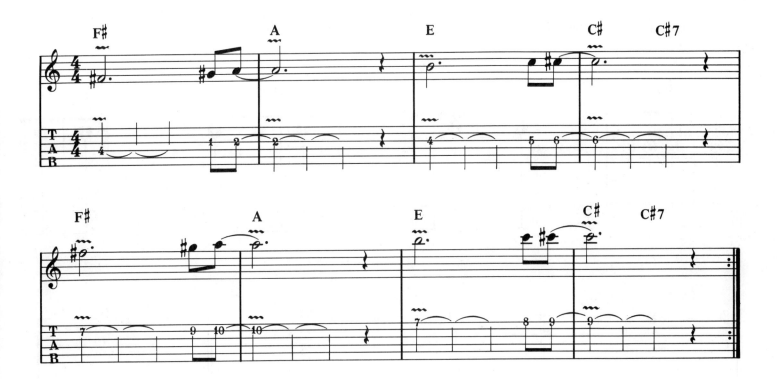

The Minor Seventh Chord

The minor seventh may also be added to a minor triad, producing a *minor seventh chord.* An A minor seventh chord is built like this: root (A), fifth (E), minor third (C)—so far an A minor triad—plus G, the note that is a minor seventh up from the root. This addition gives the minor chord a slightly softer, jazzier sound that you might hear in the music of Steely Dan. Jazz-rock fusion music and funk-soul groups such as Earth, Wind and Fire also make use of this kind of sound. I've heard it in a few rock and roll tunes too.

Like the dominant seventh, the minor seventh does not have to have all of its parts. The third and seventh are the necessary notes; the root and fifth may or may not be included, depending on the sound you want.

Don't forget that these minor seventh voicings, like most of the other chord voicings that we've covered, are movable. For example the Bb m7 on the sixth fret that follows can be moved up and down the neck to get all the other minor sevenths. (The chord on the eighth fret is Cm7, second fret F# m7, etc.) If you are aware of the position of the root in a voicing (usually on the fifth or sixth string) you'll always be able to move the chord around. Learn the names of the notes on the neck!

Let's take a look at some voicings.

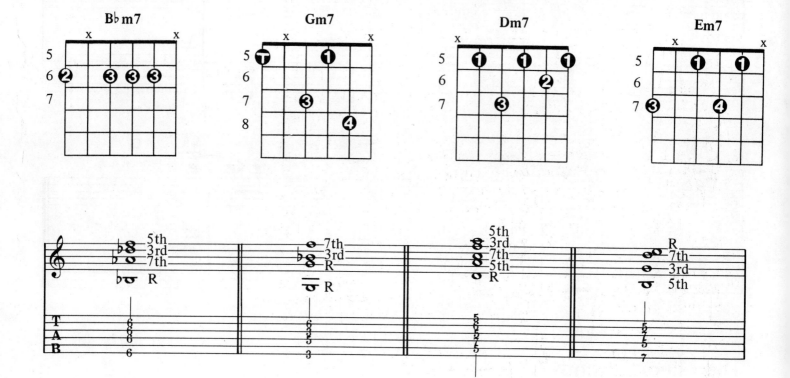

Voicing in Progressions

I've talked a lot about movable chord voicings, but we don't want to ignore "open" voicings. Open voicings utilize one or more open strings. Although they are only good in one position and can't be moved up or down the neck like some of the other chords we've talked about, there are certain situations where they work very well.

The next example is a chord progression that includes a minor seventh chord in open position. This is the progression heard throughout most of Neil Young's haunting song, "Down By the River." I've written out a lead guitar part to go along with the spirit of the song. It's a long, slow melody made up mostly of chord tones. These chord tones resolve as the chords change. We've talked about chords resolving—well, individual notes resolve too. Play through the melody and notice how the D in the first measure seems to find it's way so naturally to C♯ in the second measure. (You'll probably need a friend or tape recorder to play chords while you play the melody.) What's happening is that the D in the melody is the seventh chord, and this minor seventh naturally resolves *down* to C♯, the third of the A chord. The whole lead part is made up of chord tones which resolve to one another. In the fifth measure we see that the G (the third of the Em7) is moving down to E in the next measure. But before it can reach E it passes through F♯ . This F♯ is called a *passing tone*.

Every note in this melody has moved by step; that is, no note is separated from it's neighbor by more than a whole step. Each interval between the notes is either a half step or whole step. Many melodies move by step like this, but of course most of the time larger intervals are used to create interest. Even though our melody here contains no large interval leaps, we'll bring it alive by using some rock and roll effects such as vibrato, hammer-ons (indicated by the "H" in the music) and bends ("BU," bend up). To play the bend in this lead part, finger the note in parentheses, then pluck the string and quickly bend the string until you get the sound indicated by the note. In this case we are fingering E and bending it up until it sounds F♯. Like vibrato, this effect takes practice but is well worth learning. Just listen to all the bending that rock players do and how it sounds. The bend is definitely a prime weapon in the rock and roll arsenal.

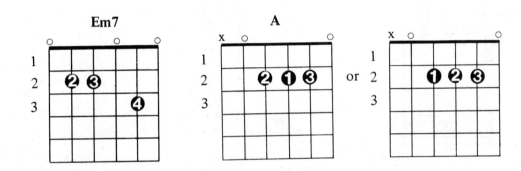

These movable voicings may also be used:

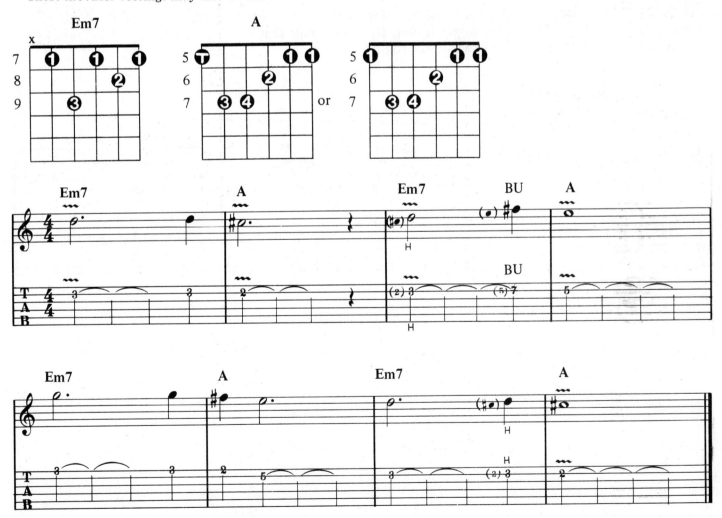

The Major Seventh Chord

We've seen how a minor seventh can be added to the major triad in order to build a dominant seventh chord. Now we're going to add a major seventh to a major triad to get another kind of chord. This is the *major seventh chord*, built by adding above a major triad the note that is a major seventh up from the root. To spell a C Major seventh chord we start with the root (C), major third (E) and perfect fifth (G). So far we have a C Major triad. We then add the major seventh, B (the note that is eleven half steps up from C). A C Major seventh is spelled C-E-G-B. A D Major seventh is spelled D (the root), F♯ (major third), A (perfect fifth) and C♯ (major seventh).

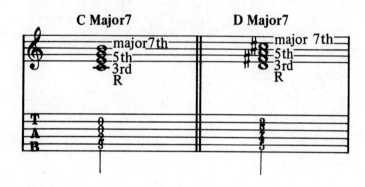

Notice that the major seventh note is found by going up eleven half steps from the root *or* one half step down from the root. To find the note that is a major seventh up from G, go down one half step to F♯.

As in other seventh chords, the major seventh has two essential notes, the third and the seventh. The root and the fifth are not absolutely necessary in a major seventh voicing. However, the characteristic sound of a major seventh chord is full and lush. To preserve this sound on the guitar, we usually use all four notes in the spelling. Some voicings:

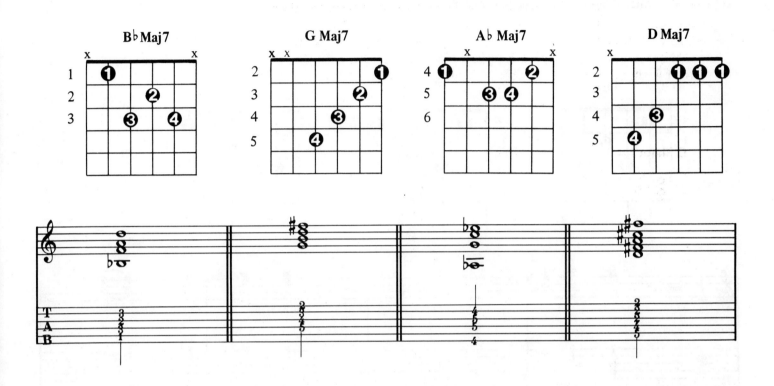

The major seventh chord has a jazzy softness that is unmistakable, once you get the sound in your ear. It might even be described as romantic and, in fact, it pops up frequently in ballads and soft rock. We find this sound in disco music, soul ballads, folk-rock, jazzy ballads and soft rock. Sometimes, the major seventh chord is used to provide a soft release in an otherwise hard-edged song. Get hold of a copy of our previous example, Neil Young's "Down By the River"; listen to it and see if you can hear where the major seventh chord comes in. Trying to hear the chord progression of a song is great practice; you should do it often for ear training and to see how song-writers use different kinds of chords. You can also learn a lot of songs this way.

Progressions with Seventh Chords

In the next example, I've written out a chord progression that includes major seventh chords and minor seventh chords. The lead part is made up of small-note voicings with chord tones and passing tones. (Try to pick out what notes of the chord are used.) It should be played with a light R&B feel—maybe something like Boz Scaggs would play.

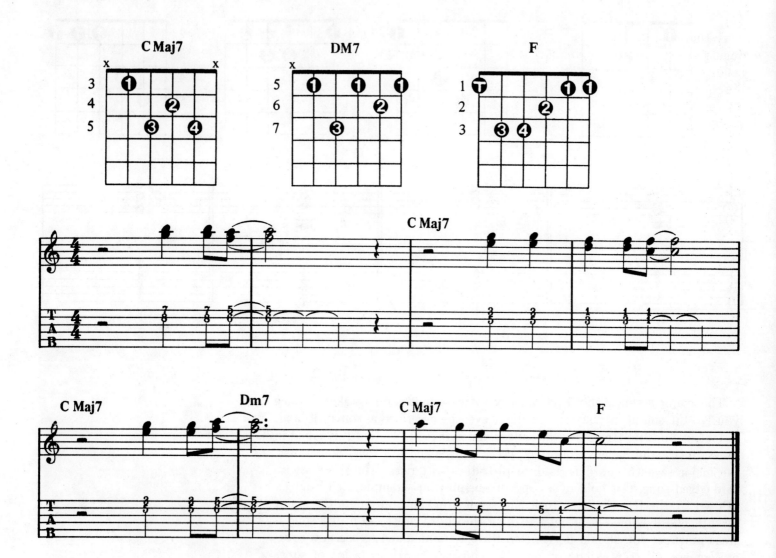

Sixth Chords

The Major Sixth Chord

The interval of the sixth may be added to a major or minor triad, producing a *sixth chord*. To spell a C6 chord (a *major sixth chord*) start with the major triad, C-E-G. To this we'll add the note that is a major sixth up from the root (eight half steps away). This note is A. So, a C6 chord is spelled C-E-G-A. F6 is spelled root (F), major third (A), perfect fifth (C) and major sixth (D).

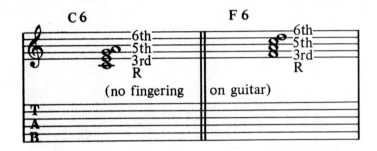

Sixth chords are rarely played on the guitar in their original form (root position) because of the adjacent fifth and sixth. To play sixth chords on the guitar we must spread the voicing out a bit. Often, the sixth replaces the fifth. (Here again, the fifth is not an essential note in a major sixth voicing.) The following voicings are very possible and sound fine. Notice the different inversions and doublings.

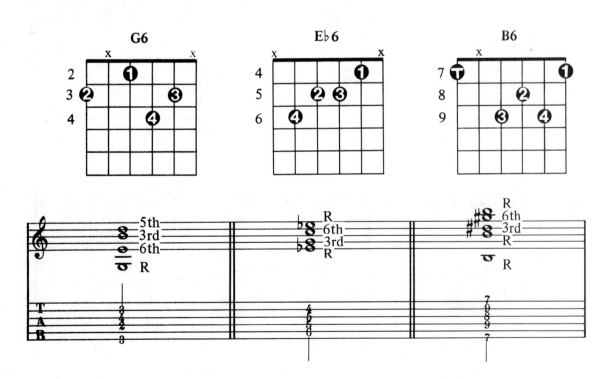

The major sixth chord has a sound that is slightly softer and jazzier than a major triad, but not as much so as a major seventh chord. It is a good compromise chord in a situation where a triad seems too blatant, and a major seventh seems too weak. The major sixth is found often in country-rock, jazz-rock and fifties rock and roll. (Listen to "Rock Around the Clock" by Bill Haley and the Comets.) The Beatles often used the sixth chord as an ending, especially in their early releases.

The next example is a dreamy ballad of the kind that John Lennon or George Harrison might play. Here we'll make use of some open voicings that really sound beautiful in this setting. Play the lead with a lot of highs (treble) but not too loud above the chords. You should try for a nice blend to get a rich, other-worldly quality. There's lots of vibrato here, and take a look at the bends in the fourth measure. The F♯ is bent up to G♯ and then bent back down to F♯. ("BU" indicates an upward bend, "BD" a downward bend.) To accomplish this, finger the F♯ on the seventh fret of the second string. Pluck the string and immediately bend the note upward to G♯. Hold the G♯ and then ease the string down as you pick it again with your right hand. The small note in parentheses is the note to be picked and fingered. The larger note is the note to be sounded.

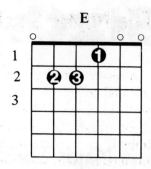

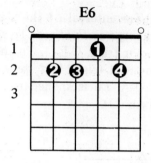

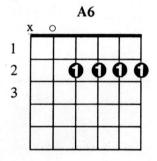
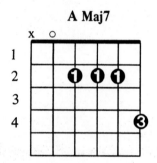
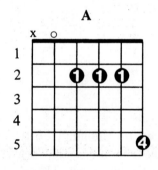
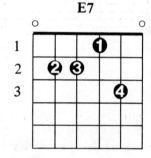

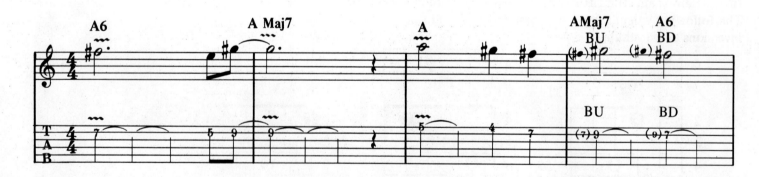

The Minor Sixth Chord

A major sixth can also be added above a minor triad. *Minor sixth chords* are used mostly as passing chords in progressions with other minor chords. We'll see some of these shortly. You should understand that a minor sixth chord consists of a minor triad with a *major* sixth interval added. (The "minor" in a minor sixth chord refers to the quality of the basic triad, not the interval that is added on.) An A minor sixth chord is spelled A (root), C (minor third), E (perfect fifth) and F♯ (a major sixth above the root). The only difference between a major sixth and a minor sixth is the quality of the third contained in the basic triad. An E minor sixth is spelled root (E), minor third (G), perfect fifth (B) and major sixth (C♯). Below we have the spellings in standard notation, but not the fingering in the tablature, again because the voicing must be spread out on the guitar.

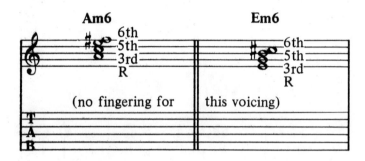

Some minor sixth voicings:

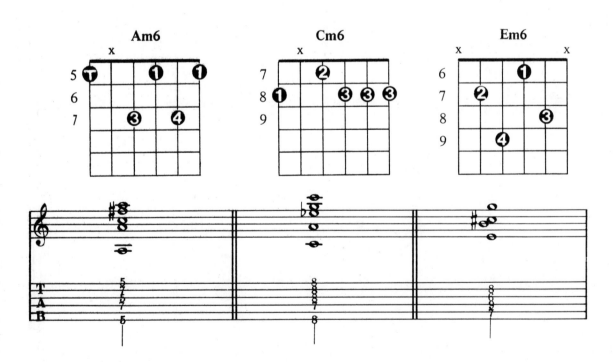

Progressions with Minor Sixth Chords

In the next two examples minor sixth chords are used as part of a basic minor pattern. Patterns like these are used often, so it's a good idea to look at them closely and get a grip on the basic idea. The idea is this: A chord progression may be constructed on a moving melody. The melodic line moves through the chords, changing them slightly each time. The movement of the line is usually by steps (half or whole). In the next example, the minor chords work in this way. In the first measure, a G that is contained in the Am7 moves down by half step to F♯, the sixth in the Am6 chord that falls in the second measure. This line continues downward as the F♯ resolves to F in the chord called "A min add F." (This means that an F is added to the A minor chord to replace E.) The F makes a final resolution to E, the fifth of the Am chord in the last measure. Notice that throughout the progression A is retained as the bass note. This A is called a *pedal tone*, a common device in rock music (and all other kinds of music). It creates tension and movement. The following chord progression is the one used by the Rolling Stones in the introduction to "Monkey Man." I've written out a lead guitar part along with the moving line of the progression. Play it at a medium, funky tempo.

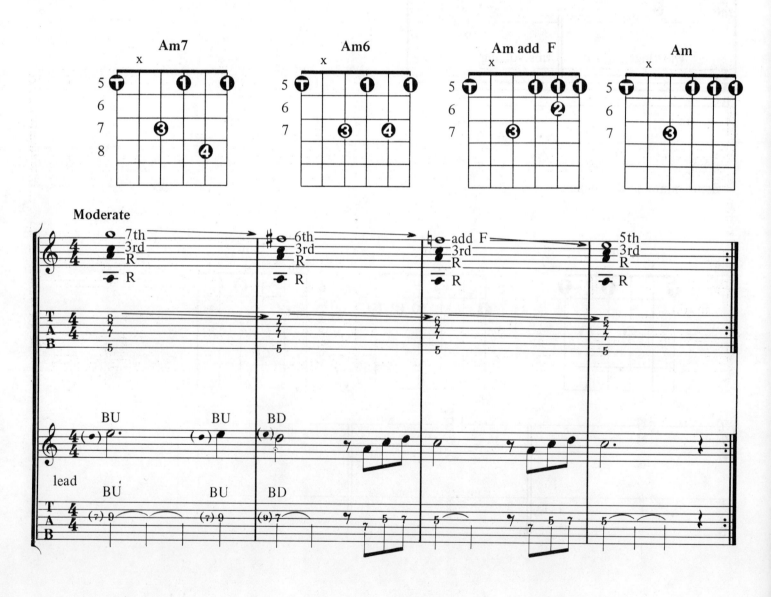

44

The next example is another minor progression built on a moving line. It is often heard in ballads like "Something" by the Beatles and "Stairway to Heaven" by Led Zeppelin. The B that is the root of the B minor chord moves to A♯ in the next measure. The chord that results is called "B min (maj 7)." It is a B minor triad with an added major seventh. You'll also see it written "B min add A♯." When the A♯ moves down by half step to the next measure, the chord that is formed is B minor seventh (a B minor chord with the added minor seventh, A). In the last measure this A resolves to G♯, the sixth in a B minor sixth chord. I've written out both a lead guitar part and a rhythm guitar part which show how the line moves through the chords.

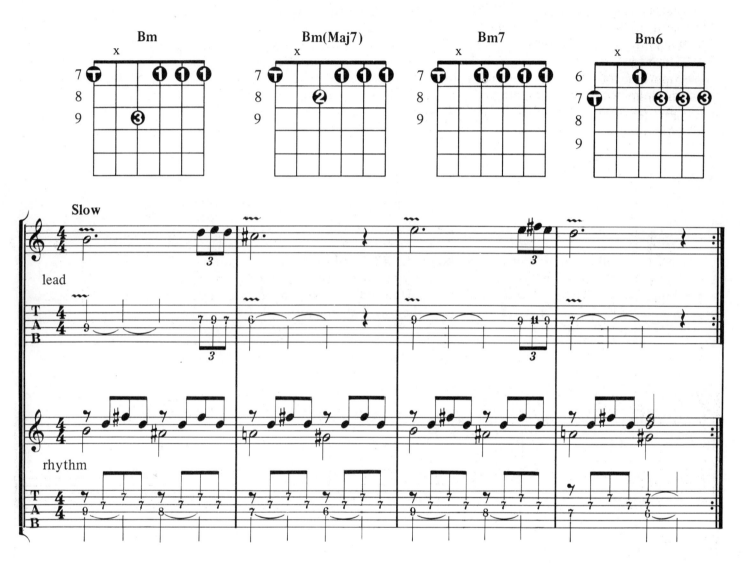

Thirteenth Chords

The note which is the sixth in a C6 chord (C-E-G-A) can also be played an octave higher. In this case, the distance from the root (C) up to A is the interval of a thirteenth. When the thirteenth is added above a dominant seventh chord we get a five-part structure called a *thirteenth chord*. A C13 is spelled C (root), E (major third), G (perfect fifth) B♭ (minor seventh) and A (a major thirteenth above the root).

When the interval of a minor thirteenth is used instead, the chord is called a *flat thirteenth chord*. A flat thirteenth chord on C, C7(♭13), is spelled C-E-G-B♭ and A♭ (a minor thirteenth above the root).

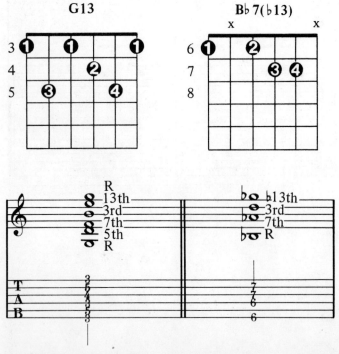

Here again not all the chord notes are necessary; the fifth and root are the most expendable. In fact, another way to think of the flat thirteenth chord is as a dominant seventh chord with a raised fifth (G♯ = A♭). When you see chord symbols such as C7(+5), C7(♯5) and C+7, these are enharmonic spellings for flat thirteenth chords.

The thirteenth chord is found in blues, jazz and western swing music. And of course any songwriter would use these chords to bring this kind of influence to a song. As a player, if you want to bring a certain "feel" to a song, you will use the chords that have that flavor. That's why it's important to understand as many different kinds of chords as you can, and to experiment with different voicings.

Play this next example with an easy, blues feeling. In the seventh and eighth measures the hammer-ons add a nice flavor. Notice that the hammered-on note is the major third of the A13. This is a standard blues articulation that you should try out on some other major and dominant seventh chords. Another interesting feature is the use of the sixths in the ninth and tenth measures. These licks are constructed by starting on the third of the chord, and going to the root using the note between as a passing tone. These lead notes are then harmonized in sixths using chord tones and passing tones. Try to relate this lick to some other keys and chords. Don't forget to try out these lead parts with a friend or cassette machine playing the rhythm parts.

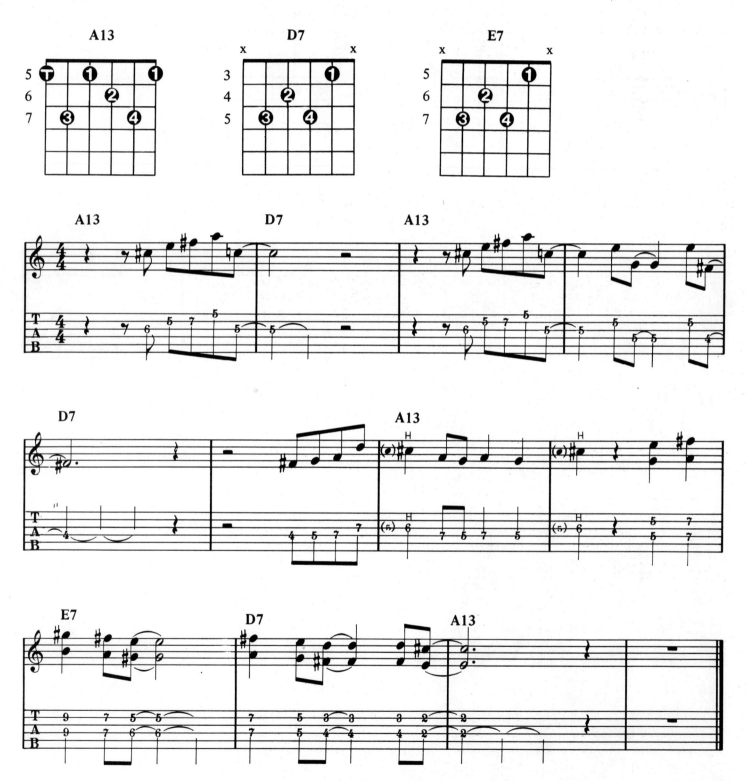

The flat thirteenth chord is very similar to the augmented triad. It is made up of the same chord tones, but has the addition of the minor seventh. The use of flat thirteenth chords and augmented triads as lead-in chords and color chords is also similar. In the next example the G7 (♭13) is used to heighten the effect of the C minor chord. Play it with a rhythm similar to the Four Tops classic "Reach Out."

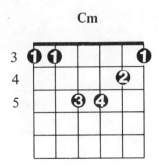

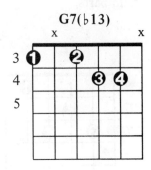

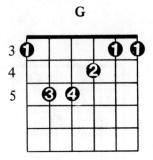

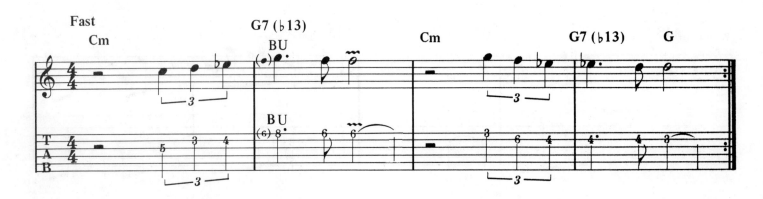

Jimi Hendrix

48

Ninth Chords

Another possible addition to major, minor and dominant chords is the ninth. The ninth, like all intervals greater than an octave, is called a *compound interval*. We have already dealt with one compound interval, the thirteenth. To find the simple interval from which a compound interval is derived, subtract 7 from the number of the compound interval. The ninth is a second plus an octave (because 9 − 2 = 7); the thirteenth is a sixth plus an octave (13 − 7 = 6).

The Major Ninth Chord

A major triad with the interval of a ninth added above it is called a *major ninth chord*. Some times the words "add nine" are used. A C Major nine chord (also called "C add nine") is spelled root (C), major third (E), perfect fifth (G), and major ninth (D). An F Major nine is spelled F-A-C-G.

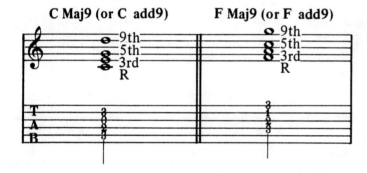

The sound of the major ninth chord is clear and steely, more austere than the sixth and the major seventh. You hear it often in folk-rock, country, progressive, fusion and rock music. The ninth is often used only for a beat or two to embellish a major chord. The Beatles made frequent use of this chord, especially in their early and middle periods. It has a ringing quality. The Byrds also made use of this sound; so did Jimi Hendrix . (Listen to "Third Stone from the Sun" on the *Are You Experienced* album.) The ninth may be combined with the sixth in the same major chord voicing to produce the jazzy sound you often hear in endings. The Beatles used to make use of this "show business" kind of ending. Or listen to the Tonight Show band.

Some voicings:

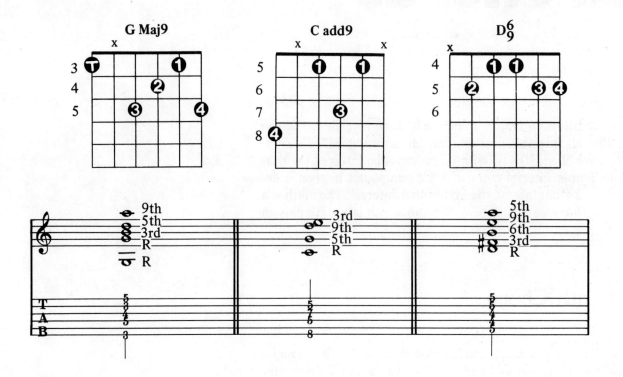

In the next example, some open ninth voicings are used. In this case a ringing, folk-rock sound is made with the rhythm voicings following the melody. This is the sound of early Beatles music. Or think of the Byrds' version of "Mr. Tamborine Man." Notice that in the D Major ninth voicing in the first and second measure, the ninth (in this case, E) actually takes the place of the third (F♯).

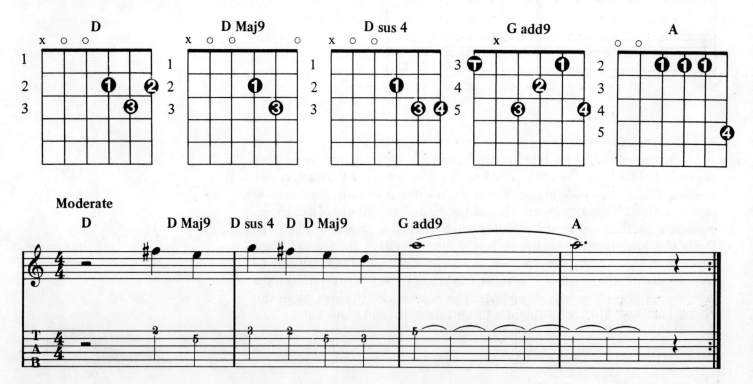

The Minor Ninth Chord

A minor triad may also have a major ninth added above it, producing the *minor ninth chord*. Most of the time, if a minor chord has a ninth, the seventh will also be in use. In some instances, however, the ninth may be used with just a minor triad. A D minor ninth is spelled root (D), minor third (F), perfect fifth (A), minor seventh (C)—so far, a minor seventh chord—and finally, the major ninth (E). A minor ninth chord may be thought of as a minor seventh chord with the addition of the major ninth. An A minor ninth is spelled A-C-E-G-B. Although the chord is called a minor ninth, it is important to remember that the "minor" in the name refers to the basic triad. The ninth that is added is a major ninth, an octave plus a major second.

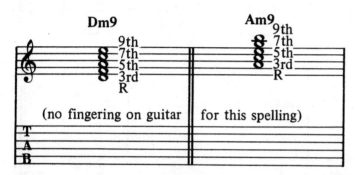

Here again , if we spell the chord in order, in a neat stacking of thirds as in the above example, fingering on the guitar becomes impossible. Simple re-arranging of the notes (different inversions) will give us some good voicings. The less important notes are the root and fifth. The third is necessary, and the seventh is used most of the time but may be left out depending on the sound you want. Of course, for that matter, any chord note may be left out or used at the discretion of the player. The aim of this book is to get you familiar with the theory of chord construction so that eventually you can make up your own voicings based on your artistic inclination. In other words, you should never lose sight of the *music* connected with particular chord constructions. O.K. Now let's listen to some minor ninth voicings.

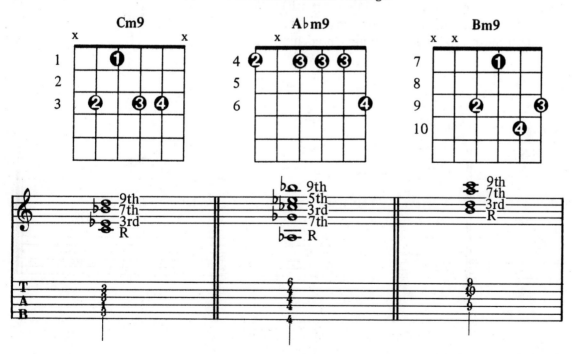

The minor ninth chord has a very smooth, lush sound. You hear it in jazz-rock, disco, mellow rock and soul ballads. Phoebe Snow, Joni Mitchell, Gato Barbieri and George Benson are some of the artists that come to mind. The following example illustrates this kind of mood. Play it with a rhythmic flow. The lead part should be strong, but not hostile.

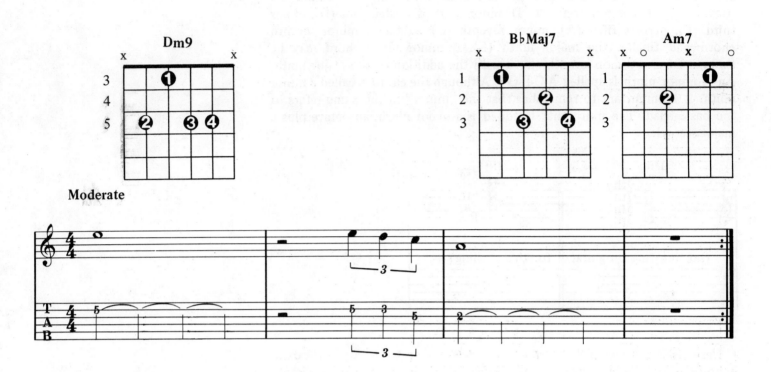

The Dominant Ninth Chord

The ninth may also be added above a dominant seventh chord, producing a *dominant ninth chord.* This gives us another five-part structure: major triad plus minor seventh plus ninth. To further complicate matters, three kinds of ninths may be used above dominant seventh chords—the major ninth, the flat ninth and the sharp ninth. A flat ninth (also called a minor ninth) is an octave plus a half step. You already are familiar with the major ninth, an octave plus a whole step. A sharp ninth (also called an augmented ninth) is an octave plus three half steps.

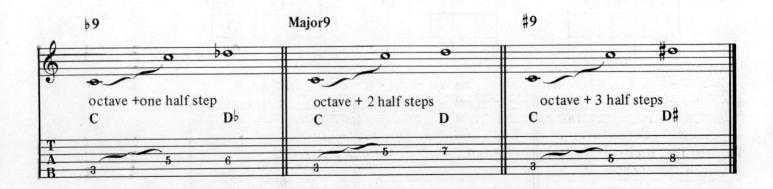

The dominant ninth chord is usually referred to simply as a *ninth chord.* So if C9 is written in the music, that means, a C7 chord with the interval of the major ninth up from the root added—D. The spelling is C-E-G-B♭ -D. An E9 is spelled root (E), major third (G♯), perfect fifth (B), minor seventh (D) and major ninth (F♯).

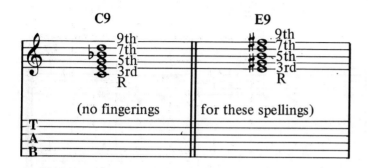

Some dominant ninth voicings:

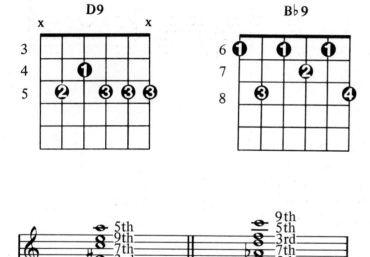

The dominant ninth is often heard as a funk device. James Brown has composed many songs based on this one chord. Earth, Wind and Fire, the Ohio Players, and the Average White Band are some other groups who have featured this chord in their compositions. Listen to the rhythm guitar part in "Pick Up the Pieces" by the AWB and you'll hear how this chord is most often used. Below we have a funk example that includes the ninth chord. The lead part is played on the bass strings of the guitar. The bass part might double this line or play an independent part.

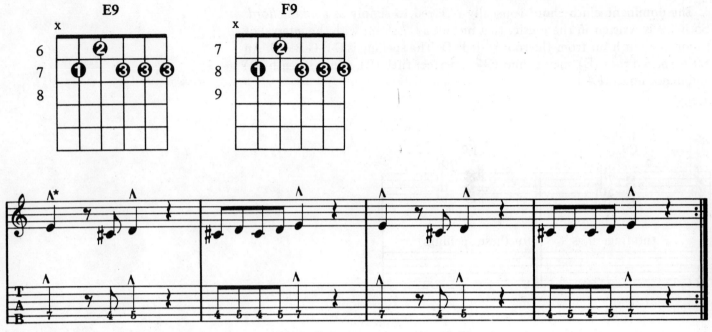

* This accent (∧) means to play the note short. "Choke" the note or mute it with the palm of your right hand.

The Sharp Ninth Chord

The *sharp ninth chord* is used in much the same way as a ninth chord. The difference between the two is the half step between a major ninth and a sharp ninth. A D sharp ninth chord is spelled D (root), F♯ (major third), A (perfect fifth), C (minor seventh) and F (sharp ninth). The characteristic sound of this sharp ninth chord is created by the tension resulting from having a major third and a sharp ninth in the same chord.

Sharp ninth voicings:

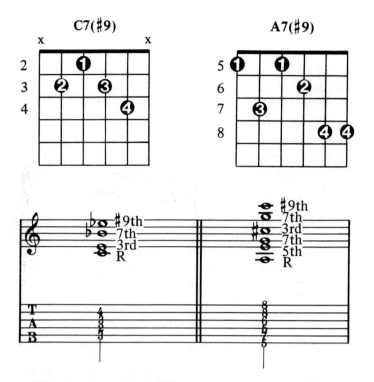

The sharp ninth chord has one of the most distinctive sounds in rock. Just think of the opening lick in Jimi Hendrix's "Foxy Lady." This is another funk-based chord, but it is often used in other contexts as an accent chord. It has a very sharp, raw and angry sound.

In the next example the sharp ninth chord is used in a progression that is similar to "Foxy Lady." The lead part features a Hendrix-style lead part with lots of bends. Notice that in the second measure the bend up is combined with vibrato. This is a touchy effect that will require a lot of practice but is well worth getting down. Hendrix was a master of this technique, and you should listen to all his recordings if you want to hear genius rock guitar playing.

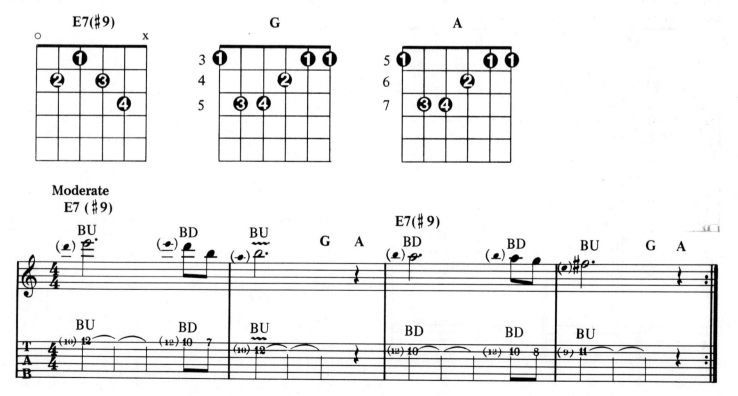

The Flat Ninth Chord

Dominant seventh chords have more possible additions than any other chord. Let's look at one more, the flat ninth. The *flat ninth chord* is a dominant seventh chord with the addition of a note that is only one half step plus an octave up from the root. The minor ninth interval creates quite a bit of tension, so this chord must be handled with care. To build a C flat ninth chord, start with the dominant seventh chord: C (root), E (major third), G (perfect fifth) and B♭ (minor seventh). Now add the flat ninth—the note that is one half step plus an octave up from the root—D♭. An A flat ninth chord is built as follows: A-C♯-E-G and B♭, the minor (or flat) ninth. You will see this chord written "A7(♭9)" or "A7-9."

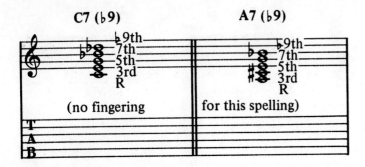

The voicings for a flat ninth chord almost always leave out the root. The fingering is exactly the same as for a diminished chord. The difference is that a diminished voicing is fingered on any note contained within the chord, and a flat ninth chord is fingered on any fret that is one half step (one fret) higher than the root of the chord. In other words, if you want to play C7 (♭9) use a diminished fingering that covers a D♭. The flat ninth is the key note in finding the voicing.

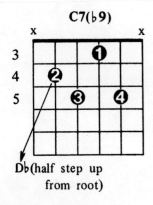

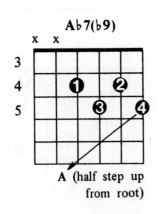

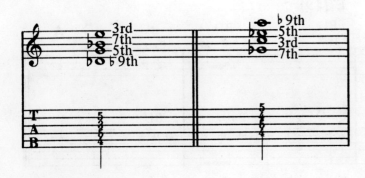

The flat ninth chord has a dark sound that is most often used before a minor chord, especially in ballads. It has a classical flavor that you might hear in the music of Yes or the Electric Light Orchestra. It is also used in a lot of slow ballads, such as those written by Elton John or George Harrison. The next example should be played as a slow rock ballad. The lead part is something that George Harrison might play with his weeping bends and metal sighs. I've written the A7 (♭9) with an optional note in the bass (the root of the chord, A) just in case you don't have a bass player at your disposal. I want you to hear this chord as A7(♭9) and not as A♯ diminished, which is how it would sound without the root.

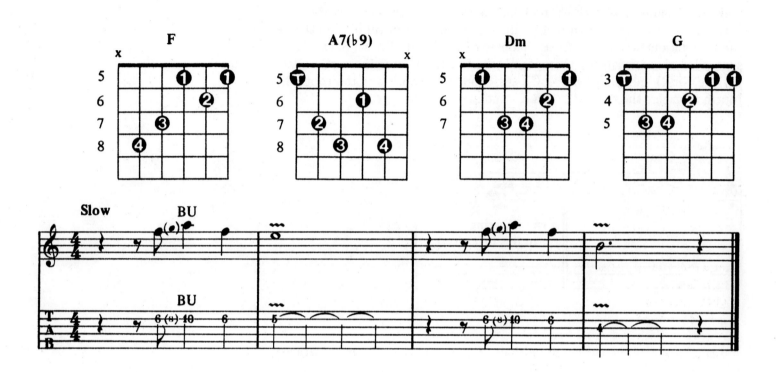

Suspended Chords

The *suspended chord*, or the *sus chord* for short, is one of the most recognizable sounds in rock. Groups such as The Who and the Rolling Stones use it so much it is almost a trademark for their sound. In a sus chord the note that is a perfect fourth up from the root takes the place of the third in a major or dominant seventh chord. This suspended fourth is usually (but not always) resolved back down to the third, creating a beautiful tension that is the foundation for such songs as "Pinball Wizard" and "Brown Sugar." A C suspended chord is spelled C (root), F (the fourth up from the root, replacing the third) and G (fifth). A C7 sus chord will consist of the root (C), fourth replacing the third(F), fifth (G) and seventh (Bb).

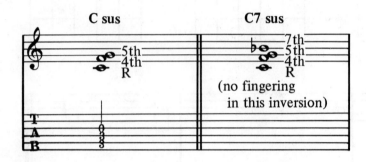

Let's look at some sus chord voicings. You may also see a "sus 4" written when this chord is indicated.

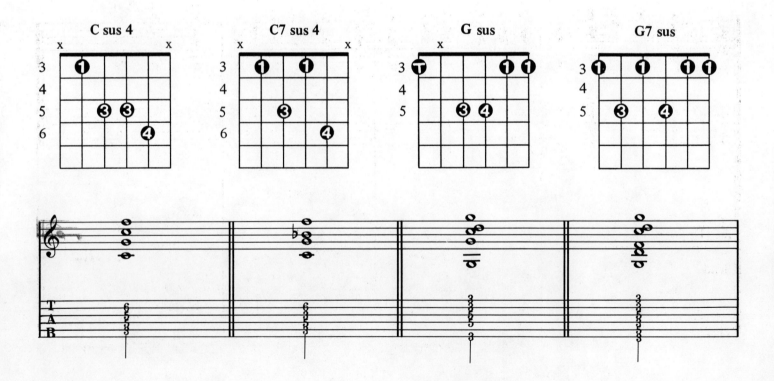

58

The next example is based on the Rolling Stones' "Gimme Shelter" from the *Let It Bleed* album. I've written out the rhythm part so you can see how the sus chord is used interchangeably with its parent major chord for color and tension. The lead part is something that Keith Richards might play over these changes.

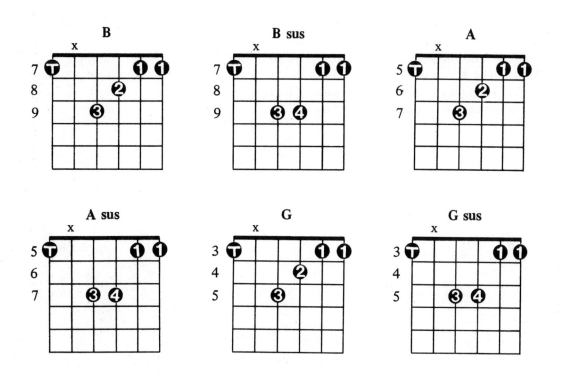

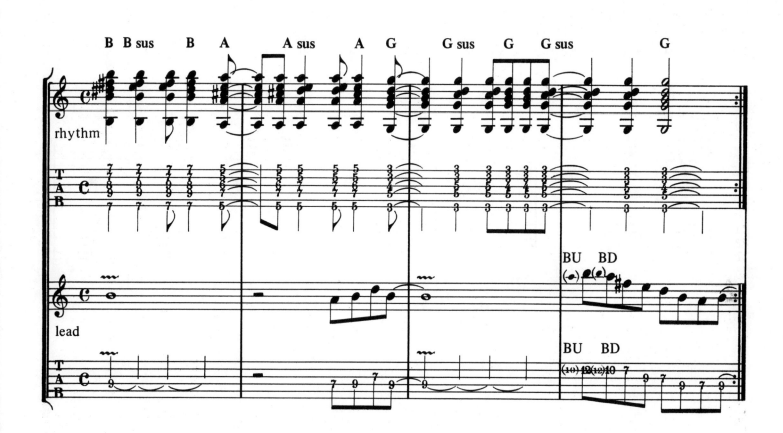

Compound Chords

Compound chords are made up of two separate parts, an upper structure and a lower structure. The upper structure is usually a triad and the lower structure is a bass note that may or may not be part of the chord. If you've ever seen a chord written "A/B" or "D/F♯" you know what I'm talking about. A/B means simply that an A triad is played over B in the bass. D/F is a triad with F♯ (the third of the chord) in the bass instead of the usual D.

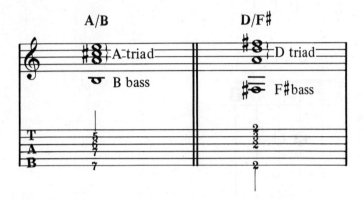

Compound chords have two main uses. First, they sound slightly different from the basic chords but still retain a familiarity that doesn't jar the ear. Second, they enable the composer to write a progression that is built on a bass line which moves stepwise. This is a technique that is used by many songwriters, such as James Taylor. He might play a bass line that goes like this:

The following example is a harmonization of this bass line using some compound chords. This may be played with a pick or with the fingers of the right hand in a classical style. It could have a folk-rock feel or even an R&B flavor like some of the songs on the *JT* album.

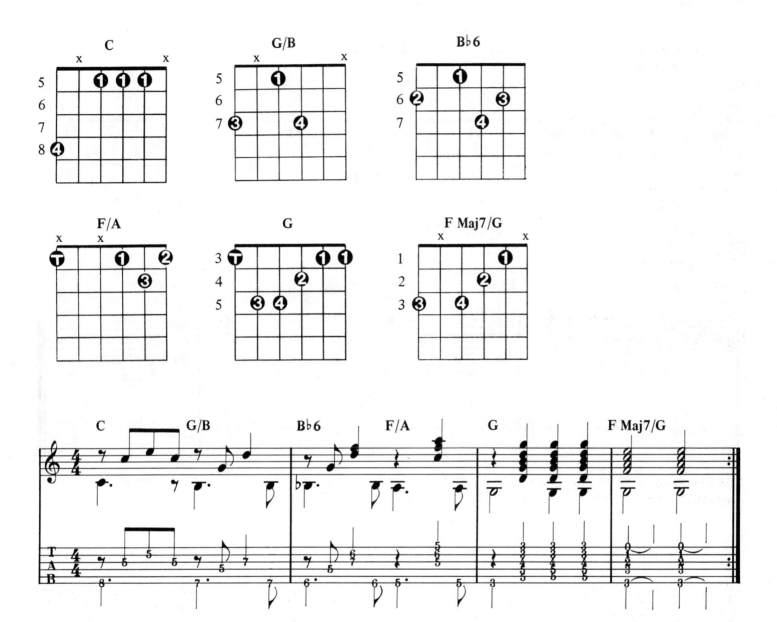

Compound chords appear often in power music (metal or fusion) played by such groups as Chick Corea and Return to Forever. One successful technique is to retain one bass note (the pedal tone that we talked about) and play different chords above it as in the following example. This has a very dramatic effect. The bass part may be played by a bass or another guitar while you play only the upper structure, or you can play the whole thing yourself.

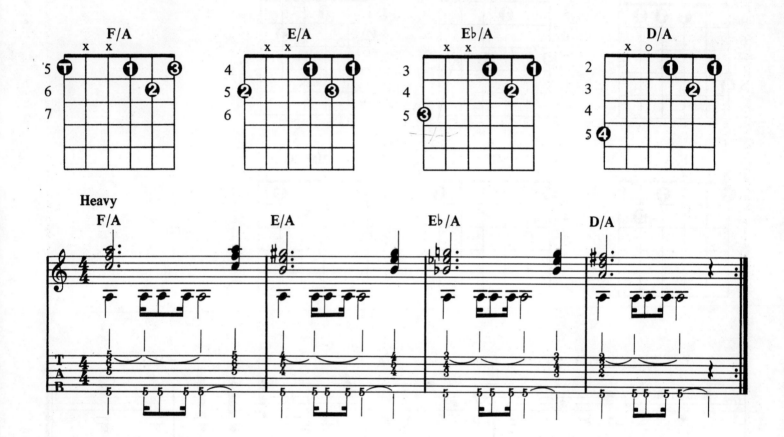

Summary

We've covered quite a bit of ground about intervals and chords, and a few other things along the way. Of course this book isn't meant to be all inclusive, and there's much more to learn about what is called "music theory." I hope you've gotten off to a good start and that you'll continue to learn and explore and create. Remember that as a musician, no matter what kind of music you play or what level you're on, you're part of a great tradition that stretches back to the beginning of music history. It's up to you to carry on as you see fit, but you've got all these thousands of years of support behind you to build on. And that includes about a quarter century of rock and roll.

The following chart summarizes what we've covered about chord construction.

Chord	Written (in C)	Basic Triad	Added	Spelling in C
major	C, CMaj	major	—	C E G
minor	Cmin, C-	minor	—	C E♭ G
augmented	CAug, C+	augmented, (root, major 3rd, raised fifth)	—	C E G♯
diminished	Cdim, C°	diminished (root, minor 3rd, flatted fifth)	—	C E♭ G♭
diminished seventh	Cdim7, C°7	diminished	diminished seventh	C E♭ G♭ A/B♭♭
dominant seventh	C7	major	minor seventh	C E G B♭
minor seventh	Cmin7, C-7	minor	minor seventh	C E♭ G B♭
major seventh	CMaj7, C△7	major	major seventh	C E G B
major sixth	C6	major	major sixth	C E G A
minor sixth	Cmin6, C-6	minor	major sixth	C E♭ G A
thirteenth	C13	major	minor seventh, thirteenth	C E G B♭ A
flat thirteenth	C7 (♭13)	augmented	minor seventh, flat thirteenth	C E A♭ B♭
major ninth	CMaj9, C add9	major	major ninth	C E G D
six–nine	C⁶₉	major	major ninth, major sixth	C E G A D
minor ninth	Cmin9, C-9	minor	minor seventh, major ninth	C E♭ G B♭ D (or C E♭ G D)
ninth	C9	major	minor seventh, major ninth	C E G B♭ D
sharp nine	C7 (♯9)	major	minor seventh, sharp ninth	C E G B♭ D♯
flat nine	C7 (♭9), C7-9	major	minor seventh, flatted ninth	C E G B♭ D♭
minor seventh, flat five	Cmin7 (♭5) C half dim, Cφ7	diminished	minor seventh	C E♭ G♭ B♭
suspended	Csus, Csus4	major, no third	perfect fourth	C F G
suspended seventh	C7 sus 4, C11	major, no third	minor seventh, perfect eleventh	C F G B♭

Appendix

Notation

Learning to read music is not difficult. Notation is the way in which musicians communicate to one another, so let's learn the language. We'll use two methods of communication: traditional music notation and guitar tablature.

Let's look at traditional notation first. On paper, music sounds are represented by written symbols called *notes*. The notes are written on a *staff* which consists of five lines and the four spaces between them.

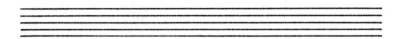

The staff is divided into *measures* or *bars* by small vertical lines called *barlines*.

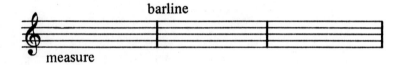

The names of the notes written on the lines are, starting with the first line, E, G, B, D, F (memory trick: Every Good Boy Does Fine). The notes in the spaces are F, A, C, E (spells the word "face").

In music notation, the *treble clef*, or *G clef* (circling the G line), is always placed at the beginning of the staff when writing for guitar.

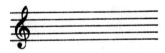

Notes which are higher or lower than those on the staff are written on *leger lines*.

Sharps and Flats

Although there are only seven letter names in the musical alphabet, there are twelve pitches in the musical octave. The other pitches are derived by the use of *sharps* and *flats*. A sharp raises the pitch one half step (one fret on the guitar) and a flat lowers the pitch one half step. A sharp or flat remains in effect until the next barline, unless it is part of a *key signature* (the group of sharps or flats which appears next to the clef at the beginning of each staff). A *natural* sign cancels the sharp or flat. All these signs are called *accidentals*.

♯ (sharp)

♭ (flat)

♮ (natural)

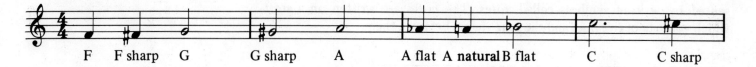

F F sharp G   G sharp   A   A flat A **natural** B flat   C   C sharp

Scales

A *scale* is any consecutive arrangement of notes, in stepwise order. A major or minor scale consists of eight notes in alphabetical sequence. Each step of the scale can also be referred to by its numerical position. For example, here is a C major scale:

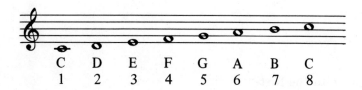

C D E F G A B C
1 2 3 4 5 6 7 8

In this case, the fourth step of the scale is F, the sixth step is A, and so on. This is how intervals are named.

Time

Rhythm and *meter* are two of the most essential aspects of the art of music. Rhythm is determined by the formation of the written note, indicating its relative duration within a measure. Meter is established at the beginning of a piece by the *time signature*. (A time signature of $\frac{4}{4}$ means that there are four quarter notes to the bar.)

In $\frac{4}{4}$ meter a whole note receives four beats, a half note gets two beats, and a quarter note (the basic unit in $\frac{4}{4}$) gets one. Most rock music is written in $\frac{4}{4}$.

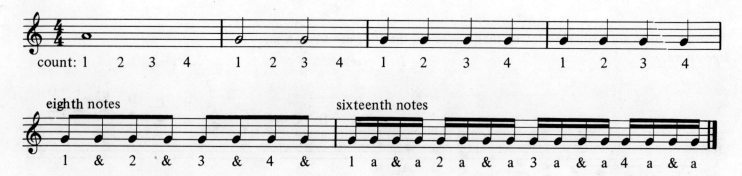

count: 1   2   3   4   1   2   3   4   1   2   3   4   1   2   3   4

eighth notes   sixteenth notes

1 & 2 & 3 & 4 &   1 a & a 2 a & a 3 a & a 4 a & a

Rests

Rests indicate a breathing space in the music. Each note value has its equivalent rest, as shown below.

| whole rest | half rest | quarter rest | eighth rest | sixteenth rest |

Ties

Ties are used to connect note values.

tie   tie

count: 1   2   3   4   1   2   3 & 4 &   1 & 2 & 3   4 &   1 & 2   3   4

Tablature

Tablature is a system of music notation that has been developed specifically for guitarists. A six-line staff is used, each line representing one of the six strings of the guitar. A number indicates which fret is to be fingered. Rests and other musical symbols are basically the same.

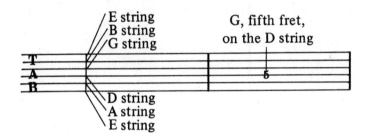

E string
B string
G string

G, fifth fret,
on the D string

D string
A string
E string

Traditional Notation and Guitar Tablature

count: 1   (2   3   4)   1   2   3   4   1 & 2 & 3   4   1   2   3 & 4 &

67

Riffs and Chords for Guitar

Blues Riffs for Guitar
by Mark Michaels

This exciting new compendium gives you hundreds of riffs in the styles of all the major blues masters. By playing and using these riffs, the blues player can gain important insights into the theory and, more important, the feel of the music; how performers like Freddie King, Albert King, Buddy Guy, Otis Rush, Eric Clapton, Mike Bloomfield, and others get that true blues emotion into their playing. Useful for beginners as well as professionals. Chord changes for all riffs are included, plus performing hints and a discography. In standard notation and tablature. $2.95

Jazz Riffs for Guitar
by Richard Boukas

Here is an important new book of guitar riffs in the styles of Django Reinhardt, Charlie Christian, Joe Pass, Wes Montgomery, Tal Farlow and others, arranged in order of difficulty. Each riff is presented with alternate fingerings for easy playing in different keys. A solo at the end of the book combines short and long phrases into a complete piece. Discography included. $2.95

Rock Riffs for Guitar
by Mark Michaels

This unique "how-to-build-riffs" approach for the electric guitar includes musical excerpts in the styles of Chuck Berry, Jeff Beck, Duane Allman and others. Special sections cover picking, fingering, bending, muting and hammering. Single and chordal riffs are all graded from easy to advanced. Discography included. $2.95

Jazz Chords for Guitar
by Richard Boukas

Here is a complete dictionary of jazz chords as used by famous guitarists like Wes Montgomery, Joe Pass, Pat Martino, Django Reinhardt and others. Organized according to "chord families," the book includes material on how to construct chord melodies, and ways to connect chords through different positions. $2.95

Available at your local music store or directly from:
Amsco Music Publishing Company, Dept. BA, 33 West 60th Street, New York 10023.
Please add 50¢ per order for postage and handling. Send for our handsome, illustrated catalog FREE.